This illuminating book, carefully researched and written, will help all Nazarenes understand their heritage.

—Dwight Gunter
Senior Pastor, Trevecca Community Church of the Nazarene

This book not only presents Bresee's story but also captures his vision of how a church should function. A must read for all Nazarenes.

—J. David McClung
Former President, Eastern Nazarene College
Owner, Naznet.com

Bangs has written the definitive biography of not only a significant Nazarene leader but also a major figure of American Protestantism. This book is essential reading for understanding our theological identity and Bresee's commitment to the poor and needy among us.

—Bob Broadbooks
USA/Canada Regional Director, Church of the Nazarene

PHINEAS
BRESEE
PASTOR TO THE PEOPLE

Carl O. Bangs
Abridged by Stan Ingersol

BEACON HILL PRESS
OF KANSAS CITY

Copyright 2013 by Beacon Hill Press of Kansas City
ISBN 978-0-8341-3005-0

Printed in the
United States of America

Abridged by Stan Ingersol

Originally published as *Phineas F. Bresee: His Life in Methodism, the Holiness Movement, and the Church of the Nazarene* in the United States of America by Beacon Hill Press of Kansas City in 1995.

Cover Design: Matt Johnson
Interior Design: Sharon Page

10 9 8 7 6 5 4 3 2 1

CONTENTS

❧

FOREWORD

*"Tradition is the living faith of the dead; traditionalism is
the dead faith of the living. Tradition lives in conversation
with the past, while remembering where we are."*
—Jaroslav Pelikan

When the belongings of C. S. Lewis went up for auction, both Wheaton and Westmont colleges purchased wardrobes from the estate. From that time forward there has been a good-natured debate between the two schools as to which one owns the particular wardrobe that inspired Lewis's vision of a passage to Narnia.

It is my current privilege as pastor of Pasadena First Church of the Nazarene to preach each Sunday from a pulpit that belonged originally to Phineas F. Bresee. There is some good-natured debate as to whether or not it was the only pulpit that belonged to Bresee or even how special this particular pulpit was to him, but in our minds the faithful in Pasadena are the true guardians of the pulpit of Bresee.

It is not surprising that after a century of development, extension into vast global contexts, and facing rapidly changing social, economic, and political landscapes, that the Church of the Nazarene would be wrestling with questions of identity. Struggling to continually redefine, recontextualize, and renarrate the core values and convictions of faith is a vital part of being a living tradition. One of the key ways that traditions thrive in the future is by reaching back and retelling the stories and celebrating the people that set the trajectory for the movement.

A living tradition, as the church historian Jaroslav Pelikan so beautifully states above, cannot simply return to its past; it has to embody it anew. It is impossible to think about recapturing the spirit of the Church of the Nazarene without examining the founding influence of Bresee. Any rearticulation of the legacy of the denomination has to take seriously his life, his passion, and his deepest convictions.

But without a thoughtful record of his life and ministry—like battles over wardrobes and pulpits—the church can often co-opt an influential leader's memory for her own purposes. In these days of frequently contested identity in the church one might wonder, who are the true "children of Bresee" today?

In 1995, Carl Bangs gave to the Church of the Nazarene an invaluable gift in the crafting of his biography of Bresee. His detailed and careful scholarship captured the fullness of Bresee's leadership and vision. But unfortunately for many people its depth and breadth also kept it from being fully accessible. And Bresee's life and work is too important to remain untouched by those who are connected to the tradition he helped to form. That is why this work that condenses and synthesizes that larger work is so important, especially for this moment, not just for the Church of the Nazarene but perhaps for the broader evangelical movement as well.

There are many things that I hope a new generation of church leaders will glean from Bresee's life as it is narrated in this revised text, but let me name just three.

First, it is my hope that in every generation the heirs of the Church of the Nazarene will be shaped by Bresee's passion for the poor. Every Nazarene should know that the denomination's name came not just from the connection to Jesus of Nazareth, but from the understanding that the word "Nazarene" had derogatory overtones (as demonstrated by Nathaniel in John 1:46: "Can anything good come from Nazareth?" [GW]). Bresee's church would be centered on Jesus the Nazarene but would also be oriented toward those marginalized persons from whom nothing good was expected to come.

In a day not unlike the day Bresee faced over a century ago, when people are still abandoning the poor in urban centers globally, the church should be reminded of statements like this from Bresee: "We can get along without rich people, but not without preaching the gospel to the poor."

Many of the faithful in the evangelical tradition since the time of Bresee have been deeply shaped by eschatologies that lack hope. In other words, the generation that currently leads the church was largely shaped by theological systems whose future expectations were that God's plan is to redeem a few out of the world before its eventual destruction. It should not surprise us that people shaped with those kinds of expectations often embody a gospel that isolates the church from the world and, like the prophet in the fourth chapter of Jonah, sits outside the city waiting for the world's great cities and cultures to be destroyed, while God is busy at work redeeming the lost of Nineveh.

So I also hope that readers of this work will pick up Bresee's very Wesleyan optimism of grace. Bresee led Nazarenes into many of the darkest corners of sin in his day because he was convinced of the transforming power of God's grace and Spirit to bring light into darkness, to bring holiness out of sin, to bring life out of death.

Finally, I also am hopeful that those who wrestle with making today's church a living reflection of Bresee's character will discover his commitment to unity on essentials while negotiating and leading an incredibly diverse group of people. It is important to remember that the Church of the Nazarene was formed more by the merging of people with similar passions and values than it was the leaving of disgruntled people from other traditions and denominations. Bresee was so devoted to the vision of holiness that many other nonessentials clearly became secondary.

In a time of rapid cultural and global changes, the questions of orthodoxy constantly rise to the surface. Technology and social media have done a lot of good things, but in the church they can often be instruments of division rather than unity. Leaders with Bresee's wisdom and conviction are desperately needed today to hold a group far more diverse than Bresee ever encountered united together around the essentials of the call to be holy as God is holy.

Bangs's work is honest in revealing Phineas Bresee as one, like all of us, with feet of clay. He was far from perfect and like all great people he was profoundly shaped by his particular moment in time. But God also used him to begin a movement that has gone far beyond what Bresee likely could have imagined. I hope that this new and very accessible account of his life will help those of us called to lead the church today to be connected with his heart so that the best days of Bresee's original vision are still out ahead of the Church of the Nazarene.

—T. Scott Daniels, Ph.D.
Pastor, First Church of the Nazarene of Pasadena

INTRODUCTION

∽

Carl Bangs's *Phineas F. Bresee: His Life in Methodism, the Holiness Movement, and the Church of the Nazarene* was published in 1995 and released at Los Angeles First Church of the Nazarene's centennial celebration in the Shrine Auditorium.

Bangs sought to reintroduce Bresee to Nazarenes. Bresee's previous biographers treated him primarily as a Nazarene founder. Bangs, though, believed that Bresee was a major figure within American evangelical Protestantism, so he set Bresee's story in its religious and theological context more completely than any of Bresee's previous biographers. He also argued that one had to know "who Bresee was as a Methodist" before he or she actually could know "who Bresee was as a Nazarene." The shift to this broader standpoint shaped Bangs's understanding of the biographer's task.

Bangs once told me that he was "an archival historian." It was not sufficient, he said, simply to analyze subjects based solely on their published works. He wanted deeper insight into their minds, which he pursued by reading their correspondence and examining other unpublished records. He used these methods to write his groundbreaking biography of Dutch theologian James Arminius, a book that brought him international recognition. It was the method he also pursued to investigate Bresee's life. Thus, over a period of years, he visited Methodist conference and congregational archives in New York, Iowa, and California, and examined materials at the Nazarene Archives, Point Loma Nazarene University, and Los Angeles First Church of the Nazarene. Likewise, he visited every farm, village, town, and city where Bresee lived and every church that he pastored.

The author's interest in his subject was deep and personal. In 1905, his parents honeymooned in Los Angeles to visit Bresee and the Church of the Nazarene there. They met Bresee again that year in Seattle and later were charter members of Seattle First Church. Bangs's sister Mildred's earliest memory was hearing Bresee preach at a district assembly, and the Bangs children grew up knowing the Northwest District's "old greats," including Elsie and DeLance Wallace, Alpin M. Bowes, and H. D. Brown, the denomination's first district superintendent. The Bangs family operated a dairy; late in life Carl Bangs still remembered that H. D. Brown's standing order included "two quarts of sour milk" delivered to his door. In college, Bangs became close with yet another Bresee associate, theologian and college president H. Orton Wiley, and in 1961 he recorded a series of interviews with Wiley. In telling Bresee's story, Bangs was always aware that his early life, his parents' married life together, his siblings' lives, and to some extent his professional life, were all influenced by people once close to Bresee.

Carl Bangs delivered the 1977 Wiley Lectures at Point Loma Nazarene University, later published as *Our Roots of Belief* (1981). His lecture on Bresee aroused great interest and led him to undertake his Bresee biography project. He was encouraged throughout by William Greathouse and Bud Lunn, and the book was dedicated to the latter.

The book now in your hand is an abridged and reedited version of that earlier work. It is published in the expectation that the author's ministry and service will be extended, and that Bresee's story will be shared by ever-wider audiences. The scholarly apparatus, including footnotes, has been dropped in this abridgment. Anyone wishing to identify the exact source of quotations appearing in this book, or to otherwise consult the author's footnotes, must go to the original work upon which it is based.

In his final months, Bresee was interviewed extensively by E. A. Girvin, a court stenographer and pastor. Girvin recorded Bresee's words verbatim, later reproducing them in *Phineas F. Bresee: A Prince in Israel* (1916). In any instance where Bangs quotes Bresee, the reader should know that he is quoting Bresee's words as published in Girvin, unless the text surrounding the quote indicates a different source, such as a sermon, public address, or publication.

—Stan Ingersol
Nazarene Archives

PART ONE
❧THE CATSKILLS☙

ONE

YOUTH

❧

Franklin and Davenport

Phineas Franklin Bresee never forgot his boyhood in the Catskill Mountains of New York. He loved the area's beauty and revisited it throughout his life.

He was born in a log cabin in rural Franklin, New York, on December 31, 1838. He lived there for one year. The cabin stood on twelve acres owned by his father, Phineas Philips Bresee. In 1840 the family moved four and a half miles to a thirty-four-acre farm, and to a house which they occupied for ten years. Bresee's formative and cherished childhood experiences occurred here. When he visited in 1907, its courteous owners threw open the house, and, he said, "We were conducted to everything reminiscent . . . the same beechtree under whose shade I rested; the same flowing spring, from whence the water still flows; the two great twin rocks upon which my sister and myself played."

Today the place is a dairy farm. The early-nineteenth-century farmhouse is still used. A beech tree stands in front. A hill is behind the house, and a large limestone slab lies in the uphill woods above the pasture. The stone, about six feet thick, was broken apart at some ancient time, leaving a passage three or four feet wide. Phineas and Diantha, his sister, played here. The "flowing spring" still flows west.

At the farmstead, one understands Bresee's enduring appreciation for nature and the beauty of his early home. To the south, he saw the roof of his home. To the west, he saw the Ouleout River valley leading to Franklin village. Bresee's parents gave him no middle name, but he later assumed one, choosing "Franklin." For him, the name surely evoked the beauty of the farmstead and surrounding meadows and forested hills, rather than the mundane Franklin village, where he never actually lived.

Phineas's boyhood was busy with farming and school. The district school was a one-room affair about one-third mile from the farm. Spelling lessons did little for him. "I could never spell," he said in 1914. "I never knew anything about grammar." His sermon manuscripts bear this out. For two winters he attended an academy in Oneonta, six miles over the mountain and across the Susquehanna River, where he studied Latin Grammar, a little algebra, geometry, trigonometry, and other rudimentary things.

Franklin presently has over a dozen structures that date from before 1850, including a charming, turreted house of early vintage that was once the place of William Miller, a lumber merchant. Bresee spoke of Miller to E. A. Girvin:

> I always felt called to preach from the time I was born . . . I remember when I was a very little boy, that the leading man in the community, who lived right down near where the turnpike road turned off from the Ouleout road, spoke to me on the subject. He was Captain Miller, a large man with a good deal of dignity. He put his hand on my head, and said: "Now what are you going to do when you are a man?" I was too embarrassed to answer, but he asked one question after another, and he said: "You will be a minister, won't you?" And I suppose there was some response in my

face. He said: "Oh, yes; that is it. That is the noblest calling of all."
And I always wondered that everybody did not know. I thought
he was smart, and that he knew that I was to be a preacher.

Phineas was twelve when the family moved in 1850 to Davenport's west edge, south of Charlotte Creek. They had a good house,
and, he remembered, "fine outbuildings, a wagon-house and barn, a
cowhouse, a cheese and milkhouse, a cornhouse, and hoghouses, all
nicely painted like a little village. The dwelling was white and all the
other buildings were trimmed in white."

The Bresee properties are clearly marked on a large county map
published in 1865 by Jay Gould, later known as a "robber baron."
Gould's map shows the "P. P. Bresee" residence on the north side of the
Davenport-Oneonta Turnpike. "School No. 15" stood across the Oneonta road, but Phineas attended little, noting: "I was getting too smart
to go to a little district school, with some young woman teacher who
didn't know as much about arithmetic and algebra as I did."

Instead, Phineas returned briefly to Franklin, taking his last
formal schooling at Delaware Literary Institute during the 1854-55
year. Bresee turned sixteen during the term. Girvin reports that the
academy was

> conducted by Doctor [George] Kerr, a man of culture, and a good
> teacher. The strain, however, of studying and doing farm work at
> the same time was too much for Phineas, and his health gave way.
> That was the end of his education, so far as regular attendance at
> school was concerned. While he attended the Franklin academy,
> he became very studious, and after that he spent much time in the
> study of Latin, Greek, and other branches.

Delaware Literary Institute was a coed preparatory school, and
its religious character was central in the early years. The institute
required students "to attend public worship twice every Sabbath."
They were to be punctual in attending prayers, and gambling was

forbidden, along with obscene language, "all use of intoxicating drinks and frequenting grog shops . . . [or] attending balls or dancing schools." The classes included botany, astronomy, physiology, French, German, chemistry, "intellectual philosophy," and thorough work in Latin and Greek. In religion, students read Alexander's *Evidences of Christianity* and Paley's *Natural Theology.* The strong emphasis on oratory yielded twenty-seven speeches delivered at one graduation exercise.

Later Bresee was diffident about his early education, yet his sermons and writings show that he was a lifelong student with a broad knowledge of science, literature, and history. And he was frequently the prime mover in establishing colleges with goals and standards not unlike the Delaware Literary Institute.

But he always had trouble with spelling.

Phineas's Conversion

The first years on the Valley Farm were spent in hard work. Around 1854, P. P. Bresee became a partner in West Davenport's general store. Bresee was required to clerk in the store, and his schooling ended. The years were marked by major turning points for Phineas. In Davenport he professed his conversion, began preaching, and made Maria Hebbard's acquaintance. The local Methodist connection was vital for the doctrines and experiences that he always valued, and for friendships.

Methodist circuit riders entered his native Delaware County after the American Revolution. Nathan Bangs was a notable circuit rider appointed in 1808, and John, Heman, and Joseph, his brothers, also served the circuit. Rev. Charles Giles recalled that the Methodists "were flourishing in the midst of opposition; zeal and diligence were leading traits in their character. They not only believed in the doctrine of holiness, but were seeking to obtain a knowledge of it by experience." He noted further: "The preaching, by which they were brought in to the kingdom of Christ, was not formal and lifeless, but close, alarming, pointed, and practical." Another observer noted that "religious services were held in the open air. . . . the prayers of the migratory Methodist preachers rang through the arches of the forest, as with plain words from honest hearts they knelt on the ground to intercede for their fellow men."

Methodist societies grew with the population. In 1823 John Bangs organized the Franklin "class," which met in a schoolhouse about a mile west of the village. William Gay, a Bresee neighbor, was the class leader. A Franklin Circuit with eight preaching points was organized in 1836, two years before Phineas's birth. The New York Annual Conference minutes show that the Franklin Circuit had 275 members in 1849. Methodist "constituents," inclusive of children, was potentially many times that number.

Davenport's early Methodist societies were on the same circuits as the Franklin societies. John Bangs organized the Davenport Center society no later than 1819. Elbert Osborn found a dispirited group in 1833—only one person attended his first sermon. A revival strengthened the work and a church building was erected. Among the many pastors, James W. Smith was the immediate instrument of Phineas's conversion, while Asahel Hough reappeared in Bresee's life thirty years later in Los Angeles.

E. A. Girvin recorded Bresee's conversion story: "In February, 1856, a protracted meeting was held in the little Methodist church, of which the parents of Doctor Bresee were members. The meeting was conducted by the pastor in charge, Rev. Smith. There were two pastors, and the name of the junior was George Hearn, a young Englishman, and an unmarried man." Rev. James W. Smith was received into the New York Conference on trial and appointed to the Franklin Circuit in 1849. He served the Davenport Circuit in 1855 and 1856. George Hearn trained for the British Methodist ministry near London, joined the New York Conference in 1855, and married an English girl in 1857. He served in the ministry until his death in 1894 and was known as a revival preacher throughout his ministry.

Girvin continues: "These two pastors held the meetings, and one day Brother Smith came to the store where Phineas was working and spoke a few words to him about his soul. This was the means of bringing him under conviction, and he determined before night that he would go to the meeting and seek salvation." One can visualize the surroundings. The church is "oriented" to the east, with the door at the west end. The road north from Davenport Turnpike and Charlotte Turnpike ran in front of the church and straight past the west side of the Bresee store. A simple act occurred: a concerned pastor walked the few hundred yards to the general store and spoke some loving, serious words to the seventeen-year-old clerk. Our story turns on that simple act.

Bresee's account continued: "I went and he preached. I thought he never would get through and give me a chance to go to the altar, but he did, finally, after preaching and exhorting. Nobody had been to the altar up to that time in the meeting, but he gave a chance and I went immediately and others followed."

The pattern was familiar. Methodism had retained three offices of ministry from its Anglican heritage: deacons, elders, and bishops. It also retained forms of worship from the *Book of Common Prayer*, which John Wesley abridged for American Methodists. And they still retained some of the Communion service forms, like the specific wording of the Lord's Prayer ("forgive us our trespasses") and the practice of kneeling for prayer.

Methodist churches also retained the Communion rail, even though Anglicanism's central altar table had given way in Methodism to the central pulpit. In the evangelistic patterns developed by

Charles Finney and others, the revival service had an "anxious seat" for "seekers" "under conviction" who went to the "mourner's bench" to confess their sin and profess new faith. Among Methodists, the altar rail became simply "the altar." Then the "mourner's bench"— originally a front pew—merged with the "altar rail." In the revival meeting at West Davenport, then, the goal was the conversion of sinners as they "went to the altar."

Bresee notes:

> The meeting continued until Sunday. I think this was Friday night. On Sunday, there was an old minister there from New York city, by the name of Lull. . . . he preached in the morning. After the morning service they had a classmeeting, which was the custom in those early days; and it was during that classmeeting that I was converted, and I realized that the peace of God came into my soul at that classmeeting.

Bresee's words are significant: the revival services prepared him for conversion, but his actual conversion was in the class meeting. The Methodist "classmeeting" was a time for personal testimony, soul-searching, and spiritual counsel. It was led by a layperson—a "class leader"—who faced the members and asked each in turn about his or her spiritual experience of the past week.

Bresee remembered his conversion not in terms of moral reform but in terms of acting on his life's vocation—the call to preach he had acknowledged since childhood. He told Girvin: "I at once began to try and do Christian work. My soul was filled with great intensity for doing the work of the Lord, and I began to hold prayermeetings, talk to and exhort the people, and do all I could to push along the work."

Smith issued him an exhorter's license, which, Bresee said, "I proceeded not to use." He was "bashful and modest." Smith made appointments for him to preach, but Phineas did not go. He finally consented to preach in spring 1857, knowing he would soon move to

Iowa. The appointment was for the Sunday afternoon service at the schoolhouse at "the Hemlocks," ordinarily George Hearn's responsibility. The school was about a mile from West Davenport. Bresee went there with Hearn. He "tried to preach" on Ps. 124:7—"Our soul is escaped as a bird out of the snare of the fowlers: the snare is broken, and we are escaped."

That was my first text and my first sermon. That is the one that I told the boys about, that embraced so much, that it had in it everything I knew. I was just a boy. It began away from before the creation of the world, came down through the Garden of Eden, along down to the fall, and down through the ages to the Incarnation and Atonement, and then on through the years until the time I was born, my conversion, then on to the judgment, and on through eternity. Although I put everything in it, it was only twenty minutes long. I wondered what in the world a fellow would ever preach about at another sermon, for I had everything in that.

When he moved to Iowa a short time later, he still had only one sermon.

TWO

HERITAGE

❧

Families

What was the relationship of Phineas's parents to the local Methodist circuits? What was their family heritage generally? What about the fact that he returned to the Davenport Circuit to marry the daughter of Horace Hebbard? And finally, what was the nature of the piety and theology that he encountered in his formative years?

Phineas described his parents as Christians and Methodists. He told Girvin: "When a very young man, Phineas Philips Bresee married Miss Susan Brown, both being earnest Christians and members of the Methodist Episcopal Church. She had removed from Connecticut to New York in her early childhood, and lived in the town of Meredith, adjoining Franklin. She was converted in her girlhood, and was a very devoted earnest Christian all her life." Susan Brown's parents had settled in Delaware County, where she was born in 1812. She married Phineas Philips Bresee at 23, about 1835.

Phineas Philips Bresee was born in Schoharie County, New York, in 1813, the youngest of "a large number of children" of Jeremiah Bresee. Jeremiah was persuaded by an older sister to allow the boy to be adopted by her and her husband, Phineas Philips, "a man of considerable standing and wealth." The aunt soon died, however, and Phineas Philips married a woman with two children. There is no clear evidence of how these developments affected the boy, nor about what relationship, if any, he kept with his birth parents.

Family tradition holds that the Bresee name is of French origin. It appears to have originated in Bressoc, a French town once occupied by Protestants. Family legends tell of people named de Bressoc fleeing France for Germany, Holland, England, and America after the persecution of French Protestants began after 1685. Family legends also tell of some branches of the family living in the American colonies before then. The name had many adaptations: Brucie, Bruzee, Bessi, Bessey, Berzie, Bresee, Brissac, and Bresac, among others. The numerous Bresees who settled in New York had first names that were common in Holland, suggesting that some of them fled France for Holland, then came to America from there. There were family branches in New York, Massachusetts, and the Niagara area of Canada. It seems true that they were of Huguenot (French Protestant) background. It is unknown when some of them became Methodists, but for Phineas Bresee's forbears, this probably occurred in Delaware County.

Jeremiah Bresee died in 1827, and Melinda, his wife, died in 1833 or 1834, so Phineas F. Bresee never met either of his natural grandparents. Bresee appreciated his early years well enough to return to Delaware County throughout his life, but his knowledge of his family background was only fragmentary. His son Ernest noted that Bresee "never talked of the family." He seemed to have no close ties to the families of his parents.

Another Davenport family was important to Bresee. The Hebbards were prominent Methodists. Horace Hebbard was baptized by John Bangs in the Davenport Center congregation in 1826. From 1840 on, Hebbard was the local Methodist society's class leader, a duty he filled for over fifty years, until his death in 1883. Hebbard supported the work of the whole circuit and was a contributor to the building fund for the Methodist church in West Davenport, three or four miles west of Davenport Center. Bresee reported that he and Nathaniel Hebbard, Horace's son, were "very warm friends." They were often in each other's homes, and Phineas grew acquainted with Nathaniel's sister, Maria.* The Hebbards had a large farmhouse on the north side of the Charlotte River, and, like many Catskills people, took in summer boarders from the eastern seaboard cities.

In 1914, Bresee remembered the family fondly:

My wife's whole family were Christians. Her father was a class leader and Sunday school superintendent. . . . He was regarded as one of the most staunch and prominent Methodists in that part of the state. My wife's mother was a very model woman. They had five children, who were all very earnest and active Methodists. The family was one of the best in that whole land, and was so regarded. They had a very nice home on a farm about half a mile from Davenport Center, overlooking the Charlotte Valley.

The Hebbards stemmed from the fountainhead of New England Puritanism. Robert Hebbard brought his wife from Salisbury, England, to Salem, Massachusetts, on the famous ship *Arabella* with Governor John Winthrop in 1630. A saltmaker, he received 640 acres from King Charles I. He was a member of the Reverend Francis Higginson's church in 1639 and died at Salem in 1684. Horace Hebbard, six generations removed from Robert, married Samantha Hoyt in October 1829. The Hebbards and all their children except Maria are buried in the Davenport Center cemetery. Maria was converted in the Davenport Center Church and testified in a Tuesday holiness meeting many years later, "I gave my heart to God at sixteen."

---

*The correct pronunciation of Maria's name is muh-RYE-uh, accenting the second syllable.

The Matrix of Bresee's Faith

Phineas found a knowledge of the gospel, an evangelical conversion, and a life's vocation of Christian ministry in Delaware County. He was born a century after the evangelical experiences of John and Charles Wesley in 1738. English Methodism was a network of "societies" within the Church of England, but the movement's evangelistic impulse moved to Ireland, Scotland, and North America, where societies formed as early as 1766. There were six hundred American Methodists by 1769, and John Wesley sent lay preachers from Britain to guide them. He sent Francis Asbury in 1771, and two years later Asbury summoned the preachers—all ten—to "confer" in Philadelphia. This first Methodist conference in America was followed by others each year afterward. The annual conference would become important to Bresee.

Methodist societies suffered during the American Revolution. Anglicans were strongest in the middle and southern colonies, but Anglican clergy were few, so that ordinary people were deprived of the sacraments. Wesley's lay preachers all returned to England, too, except Asbury. After the war, American Anglicans sought a local bishop who could ordain ministers, restore the sacraments, and allow them to participate in a church now free of the English crown.

But the Bishop of London, who had jurisdiction, refused to consecrate a bishop for America, and the pastoral needs of America's Methodists soon outweighed Wesley's Anglicanism. He concluded that irregular ordination was better than the indefinite neglect of the Lord's Supper. After careful study of Scripture and Early Church precedents, he chose Thomas Coke, an Anglican priest, laid hands on him, and consecrated him as a superintendent for the Methodist societies in America. Even more irregular, he ordained certain lay preachers as deacons and elders, and instructed them to go with Coke to America. Coke was to ordain Asbury as a deacon, elder, and fellow superintendent, and Coke and Asbury were to lead the Methodists in the new nation.

A Christmas Conference was held in Baltimore in 1784. Asbury appreciated the American democratic spirit, so he insisted that he could accede to Wesley's wishes only if the American preachers elected him to the office. They did, and he was ordained deacon, presbyter, and superintendent on three successive days. Something else happened. The American preachers were not satisfied with a mere network of societies. Instead, they organized the Methodist Episcopal Church. Coke and Asbury soon assumed the title of "bishop." With these decisions, American Methodists began charting their own course.

America's other Episcopalians did not receive their own bishop for another five years. When they did, they formed the Protestant Episcopal Church in 1789. They grew slowly, while the Methodist Episcopal Church grew rapidly. Bishop Asbury appointed Methodist preachers to large, flexible circuits that reached the largely unchurched population of the westward-moving nation. Their preaching was direct and simple: repent, be converted, and press on to Christian perfection. It was the Wesleyan-Arminian message of salvation free and full for all. Their task, as the official minutes put it, was "to reform the Continent, and spread scriptural Holiness over these lands." The last point referred to Wesley's teaching about Christian perfection in love—the "holiness" that transforms people and societies.

Francis Asbury is important in the story of Delaware County Methodism, for this evangelistic bishop penetrated the New York wilds early in his superintendency. He appointed Freeborn Garrettson to spearhead the planting of Methodism there, and the Bangs brothers were among the early circuit riders who established and nurtured the Delaware County societies. The Christian witness that shaped young Phineas is traceable to Asbury, Garrettson, the Bangs brothers, and those who worked with them. So what, specifically, did these preachers teach?

Asbury exemplified selfless endurance for the sake of the gospel. He preached repentance and conversion. He expected his hearers to be convicted of their sins and find divine forgiveness now. He also longed personally for holiness. He preached on Staten Island in November 1771: "My heart and mouth are open; only I am still sensible of my deep insufficiency, and that mostly with regard to holiness. It is true, God has given me some gifts; but what are they to holiness? It is for holiness that my spirit mourns. I want to walk constantly before God without reproof."

In May 1772 he noted in his journal: "Preached this morning at five o'clock; and this day I wrote to Mr. Wesley, and experienced a great degree of purity in my soul." In January 1773 he wrote: "Holiness is the element of my soul. My earnest prayer is that nothing contrary to holiness may live in me." And later that month: "Felt much power while preaching on perfect love. The more I speak on this subject, the more my soul is filled and drawn out in love. This doctrine has a great tendency to prevent people from settling on their lees."

In March 1779 Asbury wrote: "I was inclined to believe, that the night before the Lord had re-sanctified my soul. It afforded me much comfort; and I was ready to conclude it had been so for many years past, if I had maintained and believed it. But I fear I have been too slack in urging both myself and others diligently to seek the experience of this great and blessed gift." The theme appears again in April: "My soul was in peace; but I have not sufficiently enforced the doctrine of Christian perfection. This will press believers forward, when everything else is found insufficient; and the people in these parts appear ripe for it—for there is little or no opposition."

Asbury exhorted Freeborn Garrettson: "You will do well to press sanctification on all believers." And to Bishop Coke he wrote: "I am divinely impressed with a charge to preach sanctification in every sermon." Asbury pressed Christian perfection as a central concern of his preaching, life, and care of the Methodist movement.

How, then, did Christianity and Methodism come to Delaware County?

Delaware County's original inhabitants were the Iroquois and Lenape nations. White settlement in the area north of New York City began after the American Revolution. The Indian population seems to have disappeared entirely by 1800, and black slaves were present but not numerous. In 1810 the county had forty-four slaves in a population of 3,471 families. Slavery persisted in the county until 1818.

Church membership in the new nation was very low, and nowhere lower than on the frontier. The area's first Christian preaching was by missionary David Brainerd. Since white settlements displaced the Indians, his work left no lasting imprint there. Nathan Bangs described the situation: "A great portion of this country was entirely destitute of religious instruction . . . There were, to be sure, some small scattered congregations of Lutherans, and Dutch Reformed, along the banks of the Hudson River, and some Congregationalists and Baptists in Vermont." Congregationalists, Baptists, and Presbyterians soon entered Delaware County also. Methodism was introduced to upstate New York at Francis Asbury's behest. Methodist circuit riders staved off the more staid Congregationalists and Presbyterians, and, unlike them, invited people to accept free grace and urged them "on to perfection." They brought the discipline of their societies. The Methodist message and method took root in Delaware County.

The Bangs brothers appear repeatedly in the early histories of Franklin and Davenport. Nathan Bangs became a great Methodist editor, author, educator, and executive. His father, Lemuel Bangs, was a Revolutionary War veteran from old Puritan stock, but was, Heman wrote, "strongly attached to the Protestant Episcopal Church, and all his children were baptized in that Church." The family saw their first Methodist circuit riders in Connecticut, and Lemuel joined in the bitter opposition and ridicule accorded them. Then Jesse Lee came. Lee's learning and repartee put the mockers to shame, and his tact, piety, and message of salvation "full and free" made converts of the "hundreds of drunkards and other reprobates." Freeborn Garrettson's young men came next and formed a small Methodist society. The Bangs family regarded them as fanatics, and Nathan mocked them, but his sister, Sarah, became an important role in his conversion and that of their brother John. A few months after Nathan was converted, he was "called to preach" and received his first appointment in 1802.

He was assigned to the Delaware Circuit in 1808. There were thirty societies (or charges). The circuit covered virtually the whole county. It took four weeks to travel the entire circuit, visiting each society at least monthly. Heman joined the Methodist church under Nathan's ministry and began preaching in 1815. John entered the ministry in 1819. Joseph Bangs became a preacher in Connecticut.

The writings of Nathan and John give clear references to their preaching and teaching about sanctification. First, Nathan: "I believe the Lord sanctified my soul about six months after he justified me; but I did not always retain an evidence of it, nor live in its enjoyment, though whenever I recurred to it, either in conversation or in preaching, my heart was inflamed with divine love." In about 1838, the year of Phineas's birth, Nathan resolved to seek after the blessing. In 1848, he could say: "When I compare my present enjoyment, the inward tranquility which pervades my soul, with what had been my experience for some years, I see the difference. I cannot, indeed, describe the peace, the love, the uninterrupted communion with God, and the fellowship with all God's people which I now daily enjoy." His references to sanctification are pertinent reflections of the spiritual life that was sought. Membership in Methodist societies was not automatic, even after a profession of conversion. Converts were first received as members "on trial." John Bangs was slow to move them on to full membership, and he was disturbed when converts did not "go on to perfection." He introduced camp meetings to the circuit, and people came from miles around. In 1844, shortly before Bangs returned to serve the Davenport churches, he visited New York City to help in a "protracted meeting," reporting: "My principal object was to enforce the doctrine and experience of entire holiness with the direct witness of the Spirit."

The thread of Christian perfection became Bresee's central concern in his mature years, but other common threads were also part of young Phineas's conscious and unconscious makeup, such as the expectation that "spreading scriptural holiness" would "reform the nation." It led to serious and active concern over the issue of slavery, an economic and political institution opposed by Wesley, Asbury, Garrettson, Nathan Bangs, and Phineas Bresee. There was concern about "dram drinking," which blighted individuals, families, and society. These concerns were expressed through intense loyalty to the Methodist Episcopal Church as a disciplined company of preachers overseeing a network of disciplined Christians gathered in classes and societies. Before Phineas was five, the Methodist Episcopal Church was torn asunder by the slavery issue. The division of the churches over slavery was regarded by some as evidence that the nation would eventually divide.

The National Scene

What of the national scene during Phineas's boyhood? The United States had slightly over 17 million people when he was born. Martin

Van Buren was the president. National issues in the 1840s turned on fiscal policy, states' rights, antislavery agitation, and the acquisition of new territory (Texas, Oregon, the Mexican cession of New Mexico, Arizona, Utah, Nevada, and California). Brigham Young led the Mormons to Utah in 1846, and the California gold rush began three years later. The slavery debate was the center of attention by 1850. Like Baptists, the Methodists were divided into two denominations, one for the North and one for the South. In 1857, the year Bresee's family moved to Iowa, the Dred Scott Decision held that slaves were not citizens. Southern planters and their clergy defended slavery; abolitionists condemned it. There seemed no middle ground for an orderly, legal extension of constitutional rights to every person. The nation was headed toward war.

By the time that Phineas left the bucolic setting of the Catskills, he had been molded by Wesleyan doctrine and experience and stirred by revivals, camp meetings, and personal witness. National needs and tragedy were in the periphery of his vision when he professed his Christian faith, accepted his call to the ministry, exhorted his friends, and preached his first sermon. Not yet of voting age, he was a very new Christian and had studied no theology. When the family moved to Iowa, he was, he later observed, still "just a boy."

PART TWO
❧IOWA❧

THREE

ENTERING THE MINISTRY

⌒♋⌒

Bresee's story turns from his formative years in the Catskill Mountains to Iowa, where he spent nearly half of his preaching life. He served thirteen charges there, beginning as a frontier circuit assistant, then growing into a seasoned pastor.

In 1857, Phineas Philips Bresee sought farmland west of the Mississippi River. With Diantha's husband, Giles Cowley, he visited Iowa and bought a farm on the prairie. Cowley remained, while P. P. Bresee returned to sell his West Davenport properties. Young Phineas joined Cowley in June. Bresee told about his initial reaction to Iowa: "Oh, how beautiful the prairies looked to me in June—great stretches of them, with nothing but green grass and flowers, waving in the breezes." He and Giles worked the farm, boarding at a place "where it was hard to get enough to eat." They went out after dinner to fill up on watermelons and trout. "It was just astonishing how much fun we had that summer." His parents and sister, with their goods, arrived later that summer.

The Bresees joined the settlers who tripled Iowa's population between 1850 and 1860, pushing it to nearly 700,000. Some were foreign immigrants. Religious groups competed against one another. Methodism, with organization and zeal, soon outnumbered all other

Iowa Protestants combined. Phineas would soon be caught up in the organization and the zeal.

The farm was seven miles west of Millersburg. Churches were scarce. There was a general desire for religious meetings, so Phineas began conducting services and joined a Methodist class at Millersburg. At a quarterly conference, presiding elder William Simpson had him deliver the customary "boy preacher" sermon one evening. Afterward, Simpson "drafted" Bresee for the ministry and short-circuited some typical procedures so that Bresee could be recommended immediately to the ministry by the quarterly conference at Koszta.

The Marengo and Pella Circuits, 1857-60

Bresee was on the Iowa farm scarcely three months when he began itinerating. Bishop Edward Ames admitted him "on trial" and appointed him to assist A. C. Barnhart on the Marengo Circuit. It lay in multiple counties and took four weeks to cover all the preaching points. The Amana Colony, founded two years earlier, lay just east of Marengo.

The circuit had 207 members, two Sunday schools with sixty-five pupils, and a parsonage for Barnhart. It was a "hardscrabble circuit" and Bresee helped Barnhart by traveling, preaching, and holding protracted meetings in schoolhouses and cabins. One convert was Judge Miller, whom Bresee described as "one of the most prominent men" in Marengo. The circuit's membership increased that year by 25 percent and to seven Sunday schools with 255 pupils. Bresee's salary was $100. Barnhart's was $500. Their actual pay was $69 and $360.

Bresee began the theological reading required for ordination. He never returned to school but never quit reading. The bishops designed the course of study published in the Methodist Episcopal *Discipline*. It required exams on the Bible doctrines of "Depravity; Atonement; Repentance; Justification by Faith; Regeneration; Adoption; the Witness of the Spirit; Growth in Grace; Christian Perfection." Candidates studied English grammar, modern geography, sermon preparation and delivery, biblical criticism, general history, United States history, church history, rhetoric, logic, and the *Discipline*.

They read Richard Watson's *Theological Institutes* and *Life of John Wesley*; John Wesley's *Fifty-two Standard Sermons*, his *Notes on the Old and New Testaments*, and *A Plain Account of Christian Perfection*, with other doctrinal tracts, including his treatise on original sin; Jesse T. Peck's *The Central Idea of Christianity* (on sanctification) and *Rule of Faith*; John Fletcher's *Appeal*; and F. G. Hibbard on baptism and Palestine. Joseph Butler's *Analogy of Religion* and Nathan Bangs's four-volume *History of the Methodist Episcopal Church* were required. It would be difficult to complete the course of study and not be acquainted with the Wesleyan teaching on entire sanctification.

In September 1858, Bishop Thomas Morris sent Bresee to the Pella Circuit, where he remained for two years. Pella was forty miles southwest of his parents' farm. There was no parsonage. The year began with 160 members and 25 probationers, a church valued at one thousand dollars, and three Sunday schools with 150 pupils. Local Methodists were dominated by a Dutch-speaking colony of ultraorthodox Calvinist farmers from rural Holland, and Baptists, who gathered around their college, Central University of Iowa. Bresee called it a "half-circuit." He preached in town on Sunday morning and evening and kept afternoon appointments in the surrounding area. It was difficult. The circuit divided during the year, reducing members and Sunday school enrollment, and cutting Bresee's salary by half.

After a year, Bresee was elected to deacon's orders and to full membership in his conference. Bishop Matthew Simpson ordained him a deacon on September 12. Abraham Lincoln's friend, Simpson played a large role in national life and in Bresee's ministry.

Marriage

Bresee corresponded regularly with Nathaniel Hebbard and his sister, Maria. Phineas and Maria became engaged by letter, but her parents had misgivings. "Her mother reminded her . . . that she was of a diffident nature and slow to make warm and intimate friends," and warned that she "would be compelled to live among strangers" on the frontier. Maria thought otherwise and responded "to the dictates of her heart . . . [and] the will of her Savior."

Phineas went to New York for the wedding, held July 31, 1860, at the Hebbard home. He was twenty-two and Maria was twenty-four. Nathaniel Hebbard soon went to war, came back ill, and died. Horace Hebbard and his wife endured these losses.

The Grinnell Circuit, 1860

Phineas and Maria visited his parents' farm before proceeding to the 1860 annual conference in Oskaloosa. At conference, Bresee was on the temperance committee, which urged each minister to preach a temperance sermon annually at each point on his charge. It was a low rung on the conference ladder, but Bresee was now on it, and he would climb.

Bishop Edmund Janes appointed him to the Grinnell Circuit, which had five or six preaching points, requiring him to preach three times on Sundays. Here Bresee discovered that the plain preaching of the gospel could not be isolated from national history. Issues were convulsing the nation and bore personal costs.

Slavery was the unresolved, tragic issue that had simmered for years. There were varying attitudes toward slavery. The polarity was not merely between North and South; both regions had each extreme, and extremists scorned moderate voices. South Carolina seceded from the Union in December 1860. The Confederate States of America was formed in 1861, and Fort Sumter was fired upon on April 12.

Lincoln called for 75,000 volunteers, and the war was on. The Union army was badly repulsed at the first Battle of Bull Run. The Union was sundered apart while Bresee and his new bride were at Grinnell. America's Methodists now supported two different nations, volunteered for different armies, and rallied to different presidents.

Grinnell, its Congregational church, and Iowa College were founded by New England abolitionist Josiah Grinnell. Iowa had a Republican governor. Bresee should have found the local politics congenial. That was not the case. In his words, one appointment on his circuit "was made up largely of Southern people. They were very strong in their feeling of sympathy with the Rebellion, and I was very strong in my loyalty and anti-slavery conviction." It probably was here that Bresee draped the American flag over his pulpit, which the congregation considered a provocation. Bresee later noted that "I had already more or less grieved these people by my preaching of what they regarded as Abolition doctrine, and I saw that it would be very difficult for me to get along with them."

The circuit had other difficulties. His salary was not fully paid and they had trouble meeting basic needs. They "lived largely on faith," Bresee said, adding: "You would hardly believe what one sack of flour, with a few pounds of buckwheat to make pancakes, did us that year. . . . we were in debt somewhat when we left that circuit." Bresee considered debt wrong for a preacher. When admitted into conference membership, he had been asked Wesley's question: "Are you in debt so as to embarrass you in your work?"

He held revivals and the circuit grew, but Bresee asked for a new appointment after one year. His presiding elder warned that he might receive a poorer one, and he did.

Galesburg Circuit and East Des Moines, 1861-64

Bresee's first child, Ernest, was born while the 1861 Iowa Annual Conference was in session. Then, on August 25, Bishop Levi Scott ordained him an elder. He also received his new appointment. Bishops did not like young preachers offering suggestions about their appointments. Scott sent him to the newly formed Galesburg Circuit in Jasper County, "out on the prairie, without center or circumference, having no churches and no parsonage," Bresee later recounted.

Galesburg had about twenty inhabitants clustered in four or five houses. There were scattered preaching points. Its budget was $400. It was a bitter blow: less salary, no parsonage, and a new child. Bresee told Girvin: "I felt grieved about it, though I did not give any expression to the feeling. It was in going there that there came over me . . . such an awful determination to win and succeed in accomplishing something." He traded his good horse for a poor one, paying his debts with the difference so as to leave behind in Grinnell no "lack of confidence in a Methodist preacher."

The Bresees had two tiny rooms in the home of "Brother Butin." They were paid more in wheat, vegetables, and dressed hogs than in cash. Bresee's unease incited a vigorous response—an "awful determination" and "awful impulse," he later termed it.

He began revival meetings and asked for pledges of support. The revival spread to all six preaching points and lasted until spring, filling the schoolhouses where he preached. And the result? "The Lord gave me the country," Bresee said. This desperation was a turning point: "That charge did me more good than any I ever had. It broke me up, and broke through the chrysalis that was about me, and in some way taught me and impressed me that desperation, earnestness, intensity, would win, God helping, in doing God's work."

He did not neglect practical things. He partnered with a Methodist minister driven from Missouri by proslavery forces, and they farmed thirty acres of wheat together. With his proceeds, Bresee bought a pair of mules and added "a nice little buggy." He traded these for a horse, a new two-horse buggy, and fifty dollars. From there he went to a pair of fine horses and a brass-plated harness— status symbols of the time and place. Membership increased from a handful of people to 156 members and 65 probationers. By spring 1862, Bresee lived in a comfortable parsonage. "So that year," he concluded, "I had a good living, paid my debts, and went to conference with just as fine a team as you would see anywhere." This pattern recurred in southern California: aggressive revivalism coupled with "horse sense." But at times, Bresee admitted, horse sense threatened to be uppermost.

Annual conference met in September. A conference report "On the State of the Country" accused the slave states of violating "every principle on which the government was founded" and blamed them for extending slavery to new places. "It is the duty of every Christian minister to preach and labor and pray for the overthrow of this wicked rebellion," it said. It urged Lincoln to "issue a proclamation of universal emancipation." Ministers should urge their congregations to pray "for the success of our armies in the field, and the continued triumph of our navy, for the destruction of the cause of rebellion." Historians suggest that Southern churches later resisted the Holiness Movement because it was tied to Northern Methodists, who bitterly criticized them and sought advantage in their defeat. The Methodist schism over slavery was not healed until 1939.

Bresee wanted to stay on the Galesburg Circuit, but the presiding elder asked Bishop Osman Baker to appoint him to East Des Moines, the district's largest charge.

Bresee brought to this urban setting the methods he had used on rural circuits. Des Moines, with six thousand people, had a larger Methodist church on the river's west side, but it lay in the Southwestern Iowa Conference. East Des Moines's situation was desperate. The building was indebted for more than its value and few thought the church could survive. Bresee began aggressive revivalism and negotiated with the mortgage holder.

He was reappointed in 1863. Membership increased in his tenure from 91 to 133, and a new building was erected. During construction, the Sunday school superintendent, James Wright, Iowa's Secretary of State, arranged for them to worship in the state capitol building. Bresee was moving in higher circles. In 1863 Bresee's church had the second highest per capita missionary giving in the conference. Phineas and Maria each gave twenty dollars, thereby becoming "life members" of the Conference Missionary Society.

The couple "lived comfortably and rejoiced in the Lord." Lily, their second child, was born in summer 1864. They took the children to visit relatives in New York. Lily grew ill, delaying their return, and Bresee was absent from annual conference.

Presiding Elder of the Winterset District

Iowa Methodists redrew their conference boundaries that year. Bresee was placed in the Des Moines Conference. Denominational rules also changed: ministers could now remain at a charge up to three years. East Des Moines wanted Bresee back, but Bresee disagreed with the change, fearing that preachers would take three years to accomplish what they could do in two. He sought a new appointment. Bishop Janes appointed him presiding elder of the Winterset District.

Bresee learned this when he returned from New York. It was a great responsibility for a man of twenty-five, and the work was arduous. The district ranged from the Des Moines River to the Missouri River—over 130 miles. Houses could be 30 miles apart. Bresee filled the office for two years, and traveled constantly by buggy. Like Wesley, he read as he traveled. His reading included George Bancroft's *History of the United States* and John Motley's multivolume works, *History of the United Netherlands* and *The Rise of the Dutch Republic*, and many other books. His sermon manuscripts show wide acquaintance with American and world history.

Bresee held quarterly meetings on each charge. There was an early morning prayer meeting, a "love feast" at nine o'clock, then regular morning worship culminating with the Lord's Supper, where only ordained elders could officiate. Early American Methodism had many lay preachers; thus, a "presiding elder" visited each charge quarterly to provide Holy Communion. The title and office of presiding elder lay in this fact. More pastors were now elders, but the pattern persisted. Bresee had not sought to be a presiding elder but used the office for evangelistic purposes. He held evangelistic meetings "in groves and churches," and spoke on Methodist history, evangelizing and indoctrinating people in the Methodist ethos. On one occasion, he granted a preacher's license to eighteen-year-old H. D. Brown. Their fortunes later converged in the Church of the Nazarene.

Maria and the children sometimes traveled with him. On such a trip, Lily sickened and died. A local woman accompanied them on their sad journey back to Des Moines with their daughter's body. Phineas W, their next child, was born the following December.

Bresee grew ill from travel, heavy duties, and irregular eating. He did not connect his health with his spiritual condition, and underwent "an awful experience along the line of doubt." Girvin recorded his account:

> I had a big load of carnality on hand always, but it had taken the form of anger, and pride, and worldly ambition. At last, however, it took the form of doubt. . . . I had never answered the great questions of being, and of God, and of destiny and sin and atonement, and I undertook to answer these great questions. . . . I built

and rebuilt the system of faith, and laid the foundation of revelation, the atonement, the new birth, destiny, and all that, and tried to assure myself of their truth. . . . [Then] the devil or something else, would say, "Suppose it isn't so after all?" And my doubts would not be any nearer settled than they were before.

There is no evidence that Bresee understood how much his doubt was shaped by theological currents. The Calvinists at Princeton University tried to safeguard Scripture by "proving" that the Bible is inerrant. Liberal theology appealed to experience, reason, and intuition. Both were skeptical at heart and failed to understand that when one is in love, including being in love with God in Christ, "evidences" are not the central issue. Bresee was finding this true in his own experience.

FOUR

CHARITON, DES MOINES, AND COUNCIL BLUFFS

⌒⟿

Chariton

Bresee's official records in the church office at Chariton show his baptisms, marriages, burials, and class meeting rosters. His name is on a stained-glass window in the sanctuary, where morning light shines through it.

His discontent reflected a man increasingly at conflict with himself. Bresee was "on the way up" but had been driven in Galesburg by "an awful determination," an "awful impulse," "desperation," and "intensity." Earnestness produced results; results left "anger, pride, and worldly ambition" in their wake—a "big load of carnality" issuing in unrelieved doubt. His "inner history" takes us to the existential depth of human nature, which we can indicate by terms such as seriousness, anxiety, guilt, dread—terms indicating more than mere depression. His soul's drama played out on the Iowa prairies against the backdrop of Chariton, where Bishop Ames sent him.

Bresee remembered Chariton as "a pretty little city of about 3,000 inhabitants." It had "a good congregation, with some wealth, and a considerable degree of worldliness." They lived in a home where a young woman taught piano—Bresee said "to the point of distraction." They later moved to a four-room cottage. Salary was more difficult. Bresee said: "We left the charge in debt. We didn't have butter, meat, or the ordinary things. We fared very hard indeed."

One year the church grew from 119 members to 170, then dropped the next year. A quarter of the congregation was always angry at him, Bresee reckoned, but not the same quarter. The people took turns: "Folks were stirred up about tobacco, or worldliness, or something else." Wesleyan standards were clashing with new middle-class prosperity, a dynamic that increasingly shaped Bresee's ministry.

The larger battle was inward. Bresee held a revival on "one of those awful, snowy, windy nights." The crowd was small. He gave the altar call and no one responded. He collared a seeker in back but without success. Then, he says, "I turned toward the altar . . . this was my time, and I threw myself down across the altar and began to pray for myself. I had come to the point where I seemingly could not go on. My religion did not meet my needs." He recounted to Girvin: "It seemed as though I could not continue to preach with this awful question of doubt on me, and I prayed and cried to the Lord. I was ignorant of my condition. I did not understand in reference to carnality. I did not understand in reference to the provisions of the atonement. I neither knew what was the matter with me, nor what would help me."

He described this fifty years later. By then, Bresee had adopted the Holiness Movement's emphasis and terminology, with its focus on entire sanctification as a second work of grace that removed "depravity," the "carnal nature," or "inbred sin"—the tendency toward sin that abides with Christians after their regeneration. Bresee later taught that "human nature is corrupted through the Sin of our first parents, whereby every man is very far gone from original righteousness, and of his own nature inclined to evil, and that continually"—

words from the Church of England's Thirty-nine Articles of Religion via Methodism's Twenty-five Articles of Religion. He also later taught that "sanctification . . . is begun in every regenerate heart, and is consummated by a definite work of grace by which regenerated believers are made free from depravity and made possessors of the mystery of the Gospel—Christ revealed in the heart by the Holy Ghost." Bresee "did not understand in reference to carnality" at Chariton but could name it later.

Back to his experience: "But in my ignorance, the Lord helped me, drew me and impelled me, and, as I cried to him that night, he seemed to open heaven on me, and gave me, as I believe, the baptism with the Holy Ghost, though I did not know either what I needed, or what I prayed for."

The term "baptism with the Holy Ghost" arose in mid-nineteenth-century Methodist circles to interpret "entire sanctification," "perfect love," or "the second blessing." Bresee had a very important experience that night. Years later he described it in the Holiness Movement's language or imagery.

Some have disputed whether he regarded this as his "entire sanctification." The description and language applied to it in later years indicates that the answer for him was yes, corroborated by Bresee's 1892 testimony in the *Daily Christian Advocate*: "I joined the Iowa Annual Conference at the age of 18 years. A few years after[ward] I entered into the blessing of entire sanctification." The experience at Chariton fits this statement. Bresee later observed: "Nobody got sanctified but myself, and I did not know anything about it." Girvin's biography of Bresee, published in 1916, has this subtitle next to the Chariton episode: "Is Sanctified."

Why did Bresee not "know anything" about carnality? Delaware County Methodism was influenced by primitive Methodism, with its recurring attention to entire sanctification. And yet nineteenth-century Methodism's ambiguity over carnality and entire sanctification is reflected in the attitudes of the different bishops who appointed Bresee. Bishop Ames's writings do not discuss Christian holiness, but he allowed Rev. John Inskip, first president of the National Holiness Association, to leave the pastorate to become a full-time holiness evangelist in 1871. Bishop Morris introduced Bishop Hamline's book about Walter Palmer, a holiness proponent. Bishop Janes was active in the holiness revival, and Phoebe Palmer was his "close confidant" who regarded Janes's election as bishop "a major victory" for the Holiness Movement. He introduced Bishop Randolph Sinks Foster's holiness classic, *Christian Purity* (1851). Bishop Scott's interests centered on church polity, not theology.

Bresee greatly admired Matthew Simpson and helped name two institutions after him: Iowa's Simpson College and Los Angeles's Simpson Tabernacle. A towering figure, Simpson studied medicine, began preaching in 1834, taught at Allegheny College, and was president of Indiana Asbury University (now DePauw University). A vigorous abolitionist, he edited the *Western Christian Advocate*, became bishop in 1852, and president of Garrett Biblical Institute in 1859. He preached at the funeral services for Abraham Lincoln conducted in Washington, D.C., and Springfield, Illinois. He promoted home missions in California. Each endeavor influenced Bresee's life and thought.

Simpson associated with holiness leaders Phoebe Palmer and John Inskip but also maintained some distance. His journal reflects awareness of Wesley's doctrine of holiness and his own shortcomings, which he discussed with Phoebe Palmer in 1853. She was surprised that he did not claim the experience of entire sanctification. He probably never did so on her terms but was committed to a "greater devotion to God" and promoted holiness generally. His friendliness to the Holiness Movement led historian Charles Edwin Jones to classify him as a "holiness bishop." Bresee's bishops, then, had differing attitudes toward the Holiness Movement and its theology.

References to sanctification were embedded in Methodist culture. The Pastoral Address to the 1862 Iowa Conference urged Methodists to pray "for a general and genuine revival of religion this year," asking "for the outpouring of the Holy Spirit, that sinners may be convicted, mourners converted, believers sanctified, and the Church 'built up in its most holy faith.'" This vocabulary calls for Christian conversion and the sanctification of believers but does not speak of "entire sanctification as a second definite work of grace." Nor does it deny it.

Likewise, sanctification language appeared in some Methodist obituaries of the era. In 1862, it was remembered that Rev. Erasmus Coiner "professed the blessing of holiness, and exhibited it in his life, being a living example of the power of Christianity." But only two of forty obituaries sampled in the *Christian Advocate* mention holiness specifically. Nathan Hewitt "was a devoted Christian of the Wesleyan type. He was devotedly attached to the works of Watson, Wesley, Adam Clarke, and all the standards of our church . . . He was a firm believer in the doctrine of Christian holiness, and lived and died in the enjoyment of the blessing." Susan Williams "lived in the enjoyment of entire sanctification during [her last] fourteen years." Such references, once common in Methodist obituaries, were disappearing. Bresee would encounter the organized Holiness Movement in California, and then his understandings would sharpen.

In 1892, Bresee claimed to have "entered into the blessing of entire sanctification." To Girvin, he described the experience as it had seemed at the time, when he was still unaware of the Holiness Movement's literature. But he had read Wesley and early Wesleyan theologians and was personally experiencing what they had written about.

Bresee carried out his duties despite this turmoil, and the records in Chariton open windows on Methodism there. Class No. 1, Fred

Harris, leader, met at "Sabbath 3 O'clock at the Church." Its twenty-seven members included "M. E. Bresee," or Maria. Frederick Harris became a Methodist minister and left us a valuable memoir of Bresee. Class No. 2 met at church after the service. The church register lists the William Mitchells, whose son was the district's presiding elder. Initially, the Bresees lived with the Mitchells, where a daughter gave piano lessons. Bresee was never a music lover in any precise sense, and especially not there.

The church book has notations by each name: "Removed by letter," "Removed without letter," "Dismissed by letter," and "Joined Presbyterians." Death was of several grades: "Deceased," "Removed and promoted," and "Died in triumph."

Frederick Harris witnessed Bresee's revival intensity at Chariton and wrote that he "had a great passion for soul-saving and no Sunday's work seemed to satisfy him unless he had the joy of seeing some one saved." On "many a Sunday evening" Bresee would go "into his room alone, would prostrate himself before God in humiliation and sorrow because souls had not been saved."

The New York *Christian Advocate* places Bresee's methods in context. Its "Revival Items" column reported in January 1868 that New York City's Jane Street Church had "twenty-five conversions during the last week." From Plattskill, New York: "one of the most glorious revivals of religion ever witnessed in this place is now in progress in the M.E. Church. Over one hundred have already professed conversion, one half of whom are heads of families." From City Island, New York: "Twenty-three have professed conversion. The good work began by a powerful spiritual baptism of the Church." Methodists in Pekin, New York, had fifty converts in one revival, while those in Poughkeepsie rejoiced that "persons of all ages are being converted, baptized, and admitted into the Church on trial. . . . About 50 have been converted, and the altar is nightly filled with seekers." There were other "works of grace." Cameron, New York, reported that "backsliders are returning to their first love." Bresee's revival methods were well understood by Methodist contemporaries. His unique personal powers enhanced his effectiveness. He was no "throwback" to older days, nor an innovator working outside Methodism's accepted patterns.

Bertha Bresee was born in Chariton, joining brothers Ernest, seven, and Phineas, two.

Des Moines and Council Bluffs

Bresee served on various committees and was put on the Des Moines Conference Board of Education in 1865. By 1866, his abilities were at the fore. That year's assignments included conference visitor to both Cornell College and "Des Moines Conference Seminary" in Indianola, and the planning committee for a "State Convention of Methodist Episcopal Sunday Schools." He was on a committee "to secure a stove for the Mission House, New York," and the examiner for ministerial candidates in the third year of the course of study. He preached the annual conference's annual missionary sermon and the Sunday afternoon sermon at the courthouse.

Methodists were gathering into membership the greater part of those moving into Iowa. Schools arose naturally, often without central planning. Cornell College, Iowa Wesleyan University, and Upper Iowa University were Methodist colleges with clear status by the 1860s. The status was less clear for Western Iowa Collegiate Institute and Indianola Male and Female Academy.

The first was short-lived. The second struggled. Bresee chaired a committee that recommended that the school at Indianola be elevated to a well-supported four-year college. The committee presented the conference with new articles of incorporation establishing Simpson Centenary College as a full-fledged institution. "Simpson" was to honor Bishop Matthew Simpson. "Centenary" was to observe a century of American Methodism. The report passed. Bresee served on the first board of trustees under the new articles and remained on it for sixteen years. He would bear some of its heaviest burdens.

Money was an immediate problem, and Bresee was charged with raising enough to build College Hall. Money was raised, the hall was built, and today it is the college's venerable structure. Bresee was a principal founder of the school. Without his vision and hard work, it might not have survived.

Wesley Chapel, East Des Moines

Bresee called the roll at the 1868 Des Moines Annual Conference. Fifty-four members responded. Bishop Simpson presided. The conference had named a college for him and expressed its esteem for him in a resolution. Bresee had initiated both actions.

His third appointment from Simpson took him back to East Des Moines, now called Wesley Chapel. He began a series of morning meetings that first year. At one, "Mrs. E. M. Wright, a very quiet little woman, the wife of the deputy Secretary of State, suddenly entered into the experience of full salvation, and without any warning, fell over in her seat." This was taken as an instantaneous experience of entire sanctification. Girvin says that Bresee, "without realizing it, had been preaching on holiness to the best of his ability," and Mrs. Wright "had a very remarkable experience, and an unction, power, victory, and transformation, surpassing that of any other person that Dr. Bresee ever knew." We know that Bresee had direct knowledge of the Holiness Movement by this time: Mrs. Wright wrote an account of her experience, and Bresee sent it to Phoebe Palmer for publication in *The Guide to Holiness*.

Two tracks were converging. Mainline Methodism proclaimed its Wesleyan message but varied in the intensity of its concern for

Christian perfection. The other track starts with Timothy Merritt of New England, author of *The Christian's Manual: A Treatise on Christian Perfection* (1825) designed to strengthen Methodism's voice on perfection. In 1839 Merritt founded a paper called *Guide to Christian Perfection.*

In 1835, Sarah Lankford started a women's prayer meeting in her New York City home for those seeking Christian perfection. It became known as the Tuesday Meeting. Her sister, Phoebe Palmer, eventually became its leader. In 1839 men began attending the Tuesday Meeting, including Stephen Olin, president of Wesleyan University; Nathan Bangs, editor of the New York *Christian Advocate*; and Bishops Janes, Hamline, and Peck—all mainline Methodists. There were also some Congregationalists, Episcopalians, Baptists, and Friends. By the 1880s nearly two hundred similar meetings were being held in and beyond the United States.

By 1858, Palmer and her husband were holding revival meetings around the country. They even evangelized in Britain. Upon returning, they purchased Merritt's paper and renamed it the *Guide to Holiness*, which Mrs. Palmer edited. She wrote books on Christian holiness and developed emphases and incorporated vocabulary new to Methodism.

Palmers' followers held a notable camp meeting in 1867 at Vineland, New Jersey, where they organized the National Campmeeting Association for the Promotion of Holiness (later National Holiness Association). Its leaders were Methodist loyalists and opposed the radical "come-outers" who wanted new denominations based on holiness theology.

The fact that Bresee sent Mrs. Wright's sanctification narrative to Mrs. Palmer is the clearest evidence that he knew about her by 1868. She died in 1874, and Bresee probably never met her.

Council Bluffs: Broadway Church, 1870-73

In 1870, Bishop Janes appointed Bresee to "the first charge" in Council Bluffs, later named Broadway Methodist Episcopal Church. Presiding elder Joseph Knotts was behind the appointment. Born in present-day West Virginia, Knotts moved to Iowa in 1860 and was close friends with Bresee by 1870.

Council Bluffs still remembered its frontier origins. Its name stemmed from a council in 1804 between Lewis and Clark and the native population. Mormons settled there after 1844. In 1847 many were driven out violently and followed Brigham Young to Utah, but a sizable group remained. Relations between Mormons and "Gentiles" were tense. Rev. William Simpson organized the first Methodist society and attacked the frontier vices. He included the Mormons in his famous "frog sermon," likening them to the "unclean spirits like frogs" of Rev. 16:13. The Union Pacific Railroad made Council Bluffs its eastern terminus in 1863.

Henry DeLong, one of Bresee's parishioners, arrived with the Mormons but became a gambler at the Ocean Wave Saloon. An account states that "he was converted in the old Cottonwood Methodist Church on the side of the bluff in 1858, and became a shouting Methodist." When the saloon burned, he bought the site and a Methodist church was built there during Knotts's pastorate. This "well appointed and commodious" building was deeply in debt when Bresee arrived.

The newspapers noted Bresee's ministry in the city. On November 17, 1871, a "large congregation" heard him speak on "The Responsibilities and Privileges of Life in the Present Age." The reporter wrote that Bresee thought that "Council Bluffs still is a worldly, Sabbath breaking city, [yet] he sees constant moral improvement," though community problems remained from "the desperadoes" and "an apostate Mormonism."

Bresee was fond of the Methodist "love feast," a time of sharing Christian testimonies. His Christmas love feast tradition dates from at least this pastorate, if not earlier. He described the Christmas love feast held one year: "It was a Christmas Love Feast, in which all members met to congratulate each other on a steady progress of religion, and to commemorate in a proper manner the anniversary of the birth of Christ. . . . All who had a chance spoke of their Christian experience in times gone by; [and] how the cause of religion is progressing in their midst and throughout the world."

Broadway Church's congregational history states that Bresee "labored earnestly for the prosperity of the church and during his pastorate the membership was greatly increased."

Maria's parents still lived, and the family visited New York in spring 1870. Phineas officiated at the wedding of Mary Hebbard, Maria's sister. The next year Maria gave birth to Paul Horace. The following year, another child arrived, Melvin Arthur; now there were five children in the family.

The General Conference of 1872

In 1871, delegates were elected to General Conference. Bresee and Knotts were among the four clergy delegates. Bresee, at thirty-two, had received his colleagues' highest honor. In the spring they made their way to Brooklyn, New York, where General Conference would meet for one month. Phineas and Maria traveled with Knotts by way of the latter's old home in West Virginia. After their visit, Knotts's cousin named a baby son Bresee Kincaid. Later, many other boys would be named for Bresee.

Bresee was assigned to the General Conference's Committee on Itinerancy. The conference voted to "station" bishops, or specify their residence by region. Bresee requested a resident bishop for Council Bluffs. The Committee on Episcopacy approved but altered the resolution to read, "Council Bluffs or Omaha." Omaha was ultimately chosen. Bresee presented another memorial authorizing a Methodist Book Concern depository at Council Bluffs.

More significantly, Bresee secured the Iowa delegation's support for Gilbert Haven's election as bishop. This episode sheds important light on Bresee's thinking. Haven was from Massachusetts and edited *Zion's Herald*, a Methodist abolitionist paper. He had been converted at Wesleyan University, and while there attended the "African Church" in Middletown, Connecticut, becoming "Head Teacher" in its Sunday school. In a letter, Haven warned his parents that when he brought a girl home, she might be black. He became a minister, joining the New England Conference. He pushed the antislavery battle. He scorned the church's compromises before and after the Civil War, its failure to racially integrate conferences, its olive branch extended to an unrepentant South, and its lack of support for racial integration. He advocated interracial marriage as a method for destroying artificial differences. Haven wanted to spread Christian holiness over the land and "to reform the nation." He wanted the laity represented at annual and general conferences. He supported the New England Woman Suffrage Association, fought for women's equal voice in the church, supported female ordination, and endorsed Maggie Newton Van Cott, the first woman licensed to preach in the Methodist Episcopal Church.

Haven's views about reforming church and society were well known. Eight new bishops were elected in 1872, and Haven received a sizable vote on the first two ballots, but six others were elected. A coalition of black delegates and New Englanders supported Haven's election, and Bresee's memoir makes clear that the Iowa delegation supported him. Haven was elected a bishop on the third ballot, and Bresee's support may have been decisive.

Haven's issue was the practical effects of sanctification in the church as it faced prejudice and injustice. Bresee preached pointedly on slavery, as seen in a Memorial Day address: "Our government means liberty for all men, [but] the slave oligarchy rose up and said we will overthrow such a government and build a new empire, the cornerstone to be slavery. . . . There never was a more unprovoked, unjust, unholy war waged to secure a more unrighteous purpose." In a similar sermon Bresee stated: "The Church should be radical on every question that has in it human weal. The gospel is so intensely radical that it is making the church so."

FIVE

RED OAK

✑

The 1872 annual conference at Chariton affected Bresee in several ways. The death of Peter Cartwright was noted, a Methodist hero from the era of rugged pioneering—twenty years a circuit rider, fifty years a presiding elder. H. D. Brown transferred to the Northwest Iowa Conference and Bresee would meet him again in Seattle some thirty years later. Joseph Knotts requested "superannuated" status due to poor health. This was granted, releasing him to pursue other interests in and around the church, most of them involving Bresee. Another event occurred. Bishop Edward Andrews was unable to preside at one session. Bresee was chosen to preside in his stead. Other clergy recognized that he was a leader.

Red Oak, 1873-76

The following year, the three-year rule required Bresee to move. He did not have to wait, as before, to learn where he would be sent. A delegation from Red Oak came to the annual conference at Winterset and asked Bishop Thomas Bowman to send Bresee to them. Their leader promised that Bresee "would be well cared for. This promise was kept," says Girvin. "The church rented a good commodious place of residence, and made proper financial provision for the new pastor."

Bresee's starting salary at Red Oak was twelve hundred dollars, plus three hundred dollars for rent. This was important to provide for his growing family. His sister, Diantha Cowley, died soon after he moved to Red Oak. Their parents had lived with her in Council Bluffs and now moved in with Phineas, Maria, and the children. From now on, his parents followed Bresee from parsonage to parsonage until their deaths in California. They also took in their fourteen-year-old nephew, Fred Cowley, raising him with their children. The Bresee's youngest child, Susan, was born at Red Oak. The household had numbered seven in Council Bluffs. It numbered eleven when they left Red Oak.

In October 1873 Bresee conducted a ten-day "Home Campmeeting." Little had happened after ten days, so Bresee announced that meetings would continue indefinitely. After two weeks, some Sunday school children came to the altar. The meeting continued through the winter and into March. Girvin relates: "The revival took hold of the families, and the leading men of the town came under its influence. Merchants, lawyers, editors, and contractors, with their families and their employees, were converted, and outcasts and drunkards also gave their hearts to God. At the close of the meeting not less than three hundred persons had been saved."

The local newspaper published this account:

Such a jam as there has been at the M.E. Church of this place, Rev. Bresee, Pastor, nightly, for the last month or more, was never known before. The house is usually crowded to its utmost capacity long before the regular hour of commencing service. Numbers are kept away for want of room, and more or less are compelled to leave almost every night, for the same reason, on some occasions enough of the latter to make a respectable audience in any of the churches of the town.

Bresee's sermons were short and largely unprepared, consisting mostly of exhortation. The revival evolved more or less spontaneously. The goal was to see people repent and be converted. The method was the altar call. Bresee would sit after the sermon, the people would sing "one of the old hymns," and Bresee and others would "go among the people and reap for the altar" in "the old, Methodist fashion."

Nancy Radford was one of the converts. She and her husband were so attracted to Bresee that they followed him when he moved. Years later, she joined the Church of the Nazarene in Los Angeles. She dated her experience of entire sanctification to 1887.

Not all probationary members became full members. Some were dropped for "misconduct." Full members could be disciplined as well. This entry appears in the minutes: "Question: are any disorderly? Answer: Bro. Hilliker used profane language." "Bro. Redfern" was cited for "neglect of duty." They were visited, and Redfern "promised to do better."

The new members taxed the church's capacity. Plans were made in early 1874 to erect a new building. Another lot at the same intersection of Sixth and Hammond was purchased and blueprints were drawn for what Bresee described as "a large and expensive church for that country and that time."

The new building consumed most of Bresee's years in Red Oak. A contemporary atlas states that "the Methodists have in process of erection in the city one of the finest edifices west of the Mississippi River," and "the church is represented as being in a prosperous condition . . . [and] has a thriving Sabbath School in connection with it." Bresee estimated Red Oak's population when he began as not more than 2,500. Church membership rose during his tenure from 148 to 360. So how could he undertake to build "one of the finest edifices," and one costing twenty-five thousand dollars—a considerable sum in those days?

The *Red Oak Express* gave a whimsical account of the "new ritual at the Methodist church." There were three articles of belief: "Do you believe in Bresee? Do you believe in the early completion of the new Methodist church? Will you do all in your power to accomplish that result?" There was another, less innocent, means, as well. Bresee made pledges obligatory for reception into full membership. A convert, one of the "leading merchants," solicited his suppliers in Chicago and New York, who all gave subscriptions to the church!

The resulting building was an imposing brick structure of Gothic revival design and an adjoining parsonage. A large picture of it hangs in Red Oak's current United Methodist church. The pulpit from that era is nearby—the oldest surviving pulpit he is known to have used.

Bresee's leadership in the temperance movement went along with his revivalism and church building. American Methodism had followed John Wesley's rule against "drunkenness, buying or selling spirituous liquors, or drinking them, except in cases of extreme necessity" before the rule appeared in the church's *Discipline*, but its interpretation and application varied. Methodists grew active in the temperance reform movement in the 1830s. In 1869 a Methodist Communion steward, Thomas Bramwell Welch, developed a method of making sterilized grape juice for Methodist Communion services. He founded the Welch Grape Juice Company. The Methodist *Discipline* eventually ordered that "unfermented grape juice" (later "unfermented wine") be used in the Lord's Supper "whenever practicable." Bresee embraced "total abstinence." A newspaper described a rally in Red Oak in which revivalism and temperance intersected:

> Rev. Bresee addressed the meeting for about twenty minutes in his usual animated manner, against the sin of intemperance. While he would be charitable to the drinker and seller, and use no harsh language, duty compelled him to class the latter among the worst of criminals. . . . [The seller] could stand unmoved amid

scenes that would melt down the most hardened of any other class. The cries of starving children, the tears of mothers, and the beggary of husbands—all these he was proof against. A pen dipped in hell could not portray in colors sufficiently black the crime and misery entailed upon the country by the infernal traffic. He had sworn eternal enmity to alcohol, and expected to fight it as long as he lived.

So he did, though he kept Wesley's escape clause, "except in cases of extreme necessity." One wonders: what would Bresee's "harsh language" have been like?

Bresee, now recognized widely as a leader, was asked to dedicate new church buildings. Dedications usually took place on Sunday afternoons. The great climax, to which the sermon built, was raising pledges to retire the debt. The task was usually put to bishops and presiding elders. Bresee's success was in demand and he was known as "a dedicator" in Iowa and California.

He was elected as an alternate delegate to the 1876 General Conference, but it appears that he did not attend. Annual conference, though, was held that year in Red Oak. Bresee was host pastor, chaired the Committee on Public Worship, and sat on the nominating committee. His presiding elder was absent, so Bishop Foster had Bresee take his place on the cabinet and help draw up the pastoral appointments. Foster wanted to appoint Bresee presiding elder in Council Bluffs, but Bresee stated that his "call" was to pastoral ministry. He had been at Red Oak for three years, though, and had to leave. He was sent to Clarinda.

Mining Stock

From now until 1883, Bresee's ministry was intertwined with business. Joseph Knotts factored in this equation. Knotts had developed lung problems and could not preach, but he was not idle. He opened a book depository and was the agent for the Council Bluffs Tract Society. He published a Methodist paper, *The Inland Advocate*, which Bresee edited for a time. Knotts also published the *Weekly Independent* devoted to news and politics. He lost it all in a fire, and his lungs were aggravated by the struggle to save his goods. President Grant appointed him American consul to the Mexican state of Chihuahua. Knotts decided to watch for business opportunities in Mexico, and Bresee promised to join in any promising venture.

A year later, Knotts reported that, through "some of the richest men in Chihuahua," he had obtained "vast quantities of silver ore 'slag' and some of the old Mexican silver mines." The slag could be processed more efficiently and would yield more silver with modern equipment. The mines had flooded, but hydraulic equipment could make them workable. Among others, Knotts had purchased the famous La Prieta and Tajo mines in Hidalgo del Parral. Now he needed capital, so he formed a company to finance the project. The Mexican Mining Company, capitalized at twenty-five thousand dollars, was headquartered in Osceola, Iowa. Bresee was an early and large investor. According to Frederick Harris, who knew Knotts and Bresee well, Bresee had an eighty-acre tract near Indianola and some city lots near Simpson Centenary College. Evidently they were mortgaged to raise money to invest in the company.

Mining stock was put on the market. Agents—many were ministers—received a 25 percent commission "off the top." Motives are difficult to assess. Methodist salaries were meager, and ministers' widows had inadequate pensions. Preachers wanted to augment their salaries and, they believed, help investors. Some farmers purchased stock by mortgaging farms. Harris tells of a man who mortgaged his farm for four hundred dollars to invest in the company. His banker tried to dissuade him, to no avail. Twenty-five thousand dollars were raised, men and machinery were sent to Chihuahua, and the mines were restored to "first-class condition."

During Bresee's pastorate at Creston (1879-81), Knotts, Bresee, "and numerous financiers in Illinois, Iowa, Wisconsin, and Indiana became interested in other large mines in different parts of Mexico," Girvin says. Either a new company was formed (Girvin), or the old one was reorganized (Harris) to purchase the "iron mountain" of Mapimí in the state of Durango. The description fits Cerro del Mercado, "a hill 640 feet in height, composed almost wholly of iron ore."

The new company was organized in Chicago. It called in the old stock and was recapitalized at a quarter million dollars. The organizers included "capitalists of national reputation." Bresee enjoyed this stage of the project:

> We would go to Chicago, hire a large room in a hotel for our meetings, spend a week together, and have a great time. . . . They belonged to what I regard as the finest class of men in the country; men to whom people entrusted their interests, and who proved themselves worthy of such trust. . . . They did not scheme and maneuver to cheat those who confided in them out of their money. They liked to make money, but were magnificent losers.

Bresee remembered Knotts as "the dominant personality in all our meetings." The capitalists trusted him. Knotts depended on Bresee to be the enterprise's spokesman. One remembers Bresee's forceful revivalism. He could have been a corporation president. He was, in fact, the new company's president, according to Harris. Bresee's fascination with wealth and "leading men" was evident. It was reflected in his sermon manuscript on Isa. 48:17—"I am the LORD thy God which teacheth thee to profit."

Bresee claimed that his capitalist friends "did not scheme and maneuver to cheat." If so, they were the opposite of Jim Fisk and Jay Gould, who manipulated Erie Railroad stock to defraud stockholders and enrich themselves. Bresee's friends, on the contrary, were "intelligent Christians." One was a wholesale liquor dealer from Decatur, Illinois, a Lutheran. Others were Jay Cooke and Charles P. Helfenstein. There was hardly a more important financier in mid-nineteenth-century America than Cooke, who was critical in financing the North's Civil War effort. Many believed that he had saved the North through these efforts. An insider in the nation's postwar financial affairs, he was a devout evangelical Christian who tithed, made large gifts, and opposed the Anglo-Catholic movement within his own Episcopal Church.

Cooke invested broadly but was once cool toward mining, especially for small investors, saying: "Mining is not a proper subject for public speculation. . . . There is an element of risk . . . and many contingencies which the ignorant and the poor, and the public at large should not be invited to participate in." How, then, did Knotts and Bresee come to be in Chicago with Cooke, Helfenstein, and other capitalists? Cooke was there because he lost his fortune at one point but regained it in part by investing in mines near Salt Lake City. His new interests intersected with Knotts's ventures.

Bresee was now president of an enterprise that promised to make him a millionaire, a "capitalist," and a "blessing" to fellow ministers. He played a considerable role in the Parral and Mapimí operations. He and the liquor dealer traveled to Colorado to hire a metallurgist and buy machinery. He invested the heaviest in the Parral properties, which failed. The mine flooded again, destroying tools and machinery. And the Mapimí iron mountain, which involved Cooke and Helfenstein, proved "premature" due to a lack of railroads and insufficient demand for iron. Mapimí became an outstanding success later—but too late for Bresee and Knotts.

Bresee was also president of the Durango company, according to Harris. The claim is plausible: Bresee told Girvin that he had stock in all of Knotts's companies and was a director in several. Harris also tells of mines in Arizona. It is unclear how many companies existed, but Bresee did not tell Girvin of at least one. It, too, was a disaster.

The Arizona mines were owned by the Council Bluffs Gold and Silver Mining Company. According to an ad in 1881, five thousand shares had been sold and four thousand shares were still on the market. Knotts was company president. Other officers were from Red Oak or towns where Bresee had been pastor. The ad stated that the company "now owns the Peacock and the Bridgeport Mines in Aravaca mining district and the Silver Queen mine in the Oro Blanco mining district." Harris tells quite a tale. Knotts hired a man named Stacy as chief engineer in Mexico. Stacy returned to Council Bluffs after a year or two and claimed to have a silver mine in southern Arizona. He showed ore specimens, which "proved to be wonderfully rich in . . . the most valuable grade of that metal." Stacy sold the mine "to a company of men in Council Bluffs for $60,000, Brother Bresee and his father being among the purchasers." It was renamed "The Laura Mine" and stock sold at ten dollars a share. A superintendent reported that the mine showed great promise. Harris, now pastoring in Sidney, Iowa, was visited by Phineas Philips Bresee, who spent several days there and tried to sell his Laura stock. Harris later visited Council Bluffs, where P. P. Bresee, now dejected, told him that "all traces of silver ore had disappeared." Stacy, it seems, had "salted" the mine.

Was Knotts guilty of fraud? Bresee gave no evidence of it in his memoirs, nor mention any Arizona mining at all. An 1883 article on Knotts gave no hint of failure or scandal. It said that from the time of acquiring the Parral mines, "he has given almost his entire attention to silver mining not only in Mexico, but in New Mexico and Arizona, and has amassed a handsome fortune through judicious investments." Bresee blamed his personal losses on an explosion that filled the Parral mine with water, telling Girvin: "For all practical purposes it [the investment] was destroyed in an hour."

Harris tells a story more dramatic and less charitable to Knotts. Bresee grew troubled about his role in promoting the Parral operation. In 1882, he went to Chihuahua with a friend. W. S. Hooker, Bresee's presiding elder, told Harris the sequel. The day after he returned to Iowa, Bresee called for a meeting of company officers. He asked Hooker to accompany him to the Knotts home in Council Bluffs. Hooker told Harris: "I did not have the courage to ask him as to what he found at Chihuahua and he did not volunteer to tell me." They arrived at the meeting, and Bresee, "without saying anything about his visit to Chihuahua, or what he had discovered there," stood and resigned as company president. He gave the others his Parral company stock certificates, "worth on their face value many thousands of dollars, but worth in actual value not a picayune," and said he wanted nothing more to do with it. Then, "turning on his heels he walked out of the house, I [Hooker] following him. . . . Not a word passed between us as to what he had discovered or why he pursued the course he did."

Jay Cooke invested in mines and regained a great fortune. Bresee invested and lost his small savings. There were lessons for the church and for Bresee. Harris stated the first: "that was the end of one of the greatest frauds ever perpetrated on the people of Southwestern Iowa and in which hundreds of people lost every dollar they had invested . . ." It "brought disgrace and confusion to the Methodist Episcopal Church in that part of the State." Bresee stated the second lesson: "I formed the firm conviction at that time that I would never more attempt to make money but would give the remainder of my life, whatever it might be, to the preaching of the Word of God."

Bresee alluded to his trip to Mexico many years later in a sermon: "I was in the comparative desert lands for the first time; it was in

Old Mexico. We had been traveling through what seemed a dry and thirsty land, nothing but what looked to me like a desert, when as I looked up I saw tall, green, beautiful trees in the distance. I asked my companion about them and he said, 'The river is there.'"

SIX
FINAL YEARS IN IOWA

✑

Clarinda, 1876-79

Clarinda, a county seat, was similar in size to Red Oak. Its United Methodist Church preserves traces of Bresee's years there from 1876 to 1879. Bresee remembered the church as strong, with financially responsible members. He mentioned Congressman William Hepburn and William McPherrin, both lawyers. Harris's "Reminiscences" say that Hepburn was a skeptic about Knotts's mining ventures, yet there is no indication of strained relations between him and Bresee. McPherrin moved to Los Angeles and died in Bresee's home there.

The church was noted for its singing, and Bresee introduced "modern gospel songs." At Red Oak, he had employed "a song book with choruses" by Philip Phillips. This new music was a turning point for Bresee and American Protestantism generally. Phillips became the Methodist Book Concern's music editor in 1866. He composed and gathered a new genre of camp meeting songs. His *Musical Leaves* sold over a million copies, and *New Hymn and Tune Book* had wide Methodist use. Phillips sang at revivals and gave concerts. Bresee regarded the new songs as an alternative to sober, less optimistic hymnody. He used choruses in prayer meetings, particularly, interspersing songs and prayer.

Gospel songs were promoted in "institutes" and "musical conventions," where publishers taught the music and sold books and sheet music. P. P. Bliss and George Root had an institute at South Bend, Indiana. Numerous music conventions were held in Corydon, Iowa, between 1867 and 1883, and Chariton Methodists attended a convention conducted by Bliss in 1874. Bresee used Wesley hymns on Sunday morning and quoted them in sermons, but he complained that they contained too little testimony to full salvation now. Gospel songs had the optimistic note that fit his temper and time.

He told Girvin that "no especially great revival occurred" at Clarinda, "but there was good, steady growth, and a fair degree of success." Documents in Clarinda, though, give a different slant: "1876—P. F. Bresee—77-78. First year a gracious revival. Salary advanced from $1,000 to $1,500. Parsonage enlarged. He had a large family of children." Another document says that "the Rev. P. F. Brazee [sic] came and his pastorate was outstanding. He remained for three years, and had the largest revival that the church had ever experienced." Bresee was involved in mining schemes during these years, so revivalism was not uppermost in his memories of Clarinda. But his revivalism left an impression on Clarinda Methodists.

Creston, 1879-81

Creston was a growing railroad town, and railroad men were often on the road. The churches were weak, and the Methodist church was the weakest of all when Bresee arrived in 1879. His predecessor, though "faithful and laborious," was ineffective. "A younger and more active man was needed." Bresee worked "with his usual earnestness and zeal." The tiny church soon was crowded beyond capacity. Wings were added to each side of the building until it was wider than long. Further remodeling brought the church's seating capacity to four hundred people.

The church owed money all over town. Bresee sought out creditors and sometimes paid them from his own pocket. All debts were paid during his pastorate. The mining business had not yet collapsed, and Girvin states that "he had an income from sources entirely disconnected with his pastorates."

A church directory from 1891 contains a "condensed history." Methodists began preaching in Creston in 1870, and Bresee was the sixth pastor.

> Rev. P. F. Bresee, D.D., one of the strongest men Iowa Methodism has ever produced, was appointed [in 1879]. People in great numbers began flocking toward and into the church, until it was necessary to enlarge the old building and double its seating capacity. The salary was advanced from $700 to $1,200, and among the most liberal contributors toward rebuilding the old church and meeting current expenses was Brother Bresee and his family. To him more than any other pastor that has ever been in Creston is due the present standing and position of the church, not only in the city, but in the conference. At his own request, after serving the church two years, he was returned to Council Bluffs, and is now in Los Angeles, California, pastor of one of the largest churches on the coast.

Frederick Harris reports that Bresee became president of Knotts's reorganized Chihuahua mining company while in Creston. He was trusted as the well-known pastor of one of the growing churches in southwest Iowa and was "one of the most successful sellers of the stock." With his 25 percent commission taken off the top of sales, Bresee indeed had money. Harris says: "He told me with his own lips that he was making so much money that for months he had spent over $300 a month over and above his salary."

Return to Council Bluffs: Broadway Church and "Central Church"

Bresee was called back to Council Bluffs. The congregational history states that "because of his reputation as a worker and organizer and for his executive ability, Mr. Brasee [sic] was returned [to the Broadway Church] in 1881, to organize a new society and to erect a new edifice." Broadway was evidently strong enough to influence the bishop, but more was going on than a simple request. Presiding elder Hooker expressed his concerns about Council Bluffs to the annual conference:

> Council Bluffs is one of the great problems of this conference, it being the second largest city within our boundaries, with probably 20,000 population and less than 200 members of our church there resident. Churches weak—wickedness abounds, saloons and brothels on every side. People going to the devil by fast train and little effort is made to save them. No better missionary field in the world. We need men, money, and Pentecost power, and some of the greatest triumphs of our history may be achieved, if our beloved Methodism can be but aggressively engaged in this place.

Council Bluffs was still a Mormon center, but Bresee's account of the year at Broadway is sparse: "The work went on quietly but steadily, and there were conversions and a fair degree of prosperity."

Why did Bresee return to Council Bluffs? There were lofty spiritual values behind Broadway Church's "earnest request," but there was also real estate. Prominent Broadway members, along with civic leaders, wanted to launch "a new work in the southwestern and newer part of the city, the object being to put up a large, central church." These community leaders hoped to develop a subdivision in which they would invest. They conveyed their message to the conference through Knotts. A church site was obtained in 1882, during Bresee's year at Broadway. Knotts and Judge George G. Wright, a former justice of the Iowa Supreme Court and a United States senator, made the financial arrangements.

Hooker told Harris that Bresee's appointment the next year to "Central Methodist Episcopal Church"—the new church plant—was "nominal," freeing him to investigate the mines in Chihuahua. Bresee, then, was in a precarious position in 1883. The mining fiasco was coming to light, and his new "congregation" depended on a real estate subdivision not yet built. Undeterred by his uncertain finances, he rented a theater and conducted services. There were conversions. Then a calamity occurred, reported by the newspaper: "Council Bluffs. The Central Church enterprise begun by P. F. Bresee, services were held in a large hall. He was about to circulate a subscription paper for building a new church, when the great flood of June 1st destroyed much property in the city and caused such depression that the members and friends of Methodism in Council Bluffs decided to lay aside the enterprise until a more favorable time."

Bresee was now without real work until the annual conference in September. Already embarrassed by the mining fiasco, this new frustration fueled the sense that he should leave Iowa. He was not failing. He had not lost his colleagues' confidence. Methodism is a "connectional" organism; local churches are seen in larger contexts, as Bresee's leadership in the Iowa and Des Moines Conferences bears out. Our picture of the man at this point in his life is rounded out by surveying his connectional interests.

Bresee and Simpson Centenary College

Bresee was a prime agent behind Simpson Centenary College, as was Henry Sigler, an Osceola banker and fellow delegate to the 1872 General Conference. In 1871 Sigler donated 98 lots in Indianola to the college and gave an additional 110 acres of land in Clarke County. Still, college finances were a perennial problem. In 1878, Bishop Jesse

Peck, Bresee, and another minister urged delegates to retire the debt, and $10,400 was subscribed. The conference appointed three ministers, including Bresee, to solicit further funds. Three years later they reported that the college was in the black and its entire debt was underwritten.

Simpson College's trustee minutes show that Bresee opened the board's 1880 annual meeting, was appointed to the Committee on Faculty, and served on the Committees on Finance and Administration. In 1881 Bresee became one of seven "conference visitors" to the school. Their report, signed by Bresee, commended the college's progress in science, music, telegraphy, and bookkeeping, its growing collection of museum specimens, and assesses of what a Christian college should be: "Above all, the religious life of the college, the baptism of the Holy Spirit so richly shed upon the faculty and students, evidenced by the fact that 95% of the students profess our holy religion and are not only zealous in their studies but are also devout and attentive to religious duties, is an insurance of the divine favor upon the institution. Too many institutions of learning . . . [ignore] the higher and more important education, that of the heart."

The names of Sigler, Judge Wright, and Bresee appear in subsequent board meeting minutes. Wright was president in 1881 and Bresee in 1882, when Sigler was vice president. Bresee was reelected president in 1883 and not replaced until June 1884, a year after he moved to California. Wright, the new chairman, recommended that Bresee be awarded the honorary degree of doctor of divinity. Thus, after moving to California, he became "Dr. Bresee," as he was later known and remembered. The embarrassment over mining stock had not damaged the reputations of Bresee and Judge Wright.

Other Educational Concerns

Bresee never attended college or seminary but carried large responsibilities for higher education. He served on the Iowa Conference's Committee on Publications in 1863 and often thereafter; on the Des Moines Conference's Board of Education; examiner of third year candidates in the course of study; conference visitor to Cornell College; and on a committee to plan a statewide Sunday school convention. He became a Simpson College trustee in 1867, first recording secretary of the Des Moines Conference's Historical Society, conference visitor to Garrett Biblical Institute, president in 1879 of the conference Sunday School Association, and chairman of the Board of Education in 1881.

Bresee first encountered a theological seminary as conference visitor to Garrett Biblical Institute. As chairman of the Garrett visitors (an advisory group), Bresee reported in 1878 that the seminary enjoyed "unprecedented prosperity and promise," with all twenty-four recent graduates placed in regular pastorates. "The spiritual tone of the Institute was never better. The students are devotional and abundant in work." He urged his conference to extend loans to Garrett's students and welcome its graduates into their clergy ranks.

Committee work was normal for Methodist ministers, but Bresee's list was unusually weighty. His routine committee responsibilities included periodicals, missionary concerns, church extension, rules, and the office of conference secretary, among others. He was on the Board of Triers of Appeals, on a commission to redefine conference boundaries, on an advisory board on the sale of church property. He was on committees to select Simpson College's president, select an episcopal residence in Des Moines, and study Mormonism. He preached several times to the conference and gave its missionary address. He edited the conference paper for a time. Twice Bresee presided over annual conference sessions in the absence of a bishop;

no other minister was chosen to do this during Bresee's years in the Iowa and Des Moines conferences.

He was in demand to dedicate new church buildings. A news report tells why: "After three years of labor, the new edifice at Dunlap is so far finished that it can be occupied, and it was dedicated July 9th. Rev. P. F. Bresee, of Council Bluffs, preached, and succeeded in raising a little over one thousand dollars to meet a balance of $930.28." Bresee's preaching was eloquent and persuasive. A few months later, "the new church at Silver City was dedicated January 7th, by Rev. P. H. [sic] Bresee, of Council Bluffs." Bresee was dedicating churches as early as his Red Oak pastorate.

There was almost no slot in the conference structure that Bresee had not filled by the time he left Iowa. He was often a committee's secretary or chairman. He had attended neither college nor seminary but was well trained in practical theology and church administration during his Iowa years.

Bresee's Self-understanding in Iowa

Bresee carried administrative responsibilities, but his ministry did not center on management. He never sought to be a presiding elder, nor did he ever remain in the office for the full three years. He was a pastor at his core. He expressed this at a statewide Methodist meeting in 1881, where he spoke on "The Pastoral Office." Other addresses dealt with procedures. Bresee made another point entirely.

The details of the pastoral office were not as important, he said, as being "an efficient agent through whom the Holy Spirit may work." A pastor's work "embraces all departments of Christian ministry." First, the pastor is an evangelist working in that "large borderland where the Church and the world meet and mingle, where those who are not Christians, yet permeated largely with Christian thought and Christian principles, sit in our sanctuaries and abide in our homes." Others outside that circle "are devoid of all Christian life," so churches and pastors have their first responsibility there, he said. "The pastor must always be evangelistic. It would seem to be a poor ministry of the gospel of Jesus Christ that was not an evangel to unsaved men. It would seem a very barren ministry that gathered no souls to the crop." Evangelism was the pastor's responsibility. "No special evangelist can take the place or do this work for the pastor."

Second, Bresee asserted that the pastor was a "teacher of the Word of Truth to the whole Church. . . . a seer . . . his gaze is further in the azure and deeper into the depths of truth, especially such truth as pertains to the redemption, salvation and perfection of the souls of men." There are "unexplored depths" everywhere. Only when the pastor senses their infinite glory can they be taught effectively to others.

Third, the pastor was "a perennial fountain of moral influence and power." The pastor's proclamation and teaching must be infused with "a moral power which makes his own unseen life draw men and impel them with its own power towards Christ and heaven." A person, he said, "who, seeing truth is not thrilled by it . . . is not fitted to be a Christian teacher . . . A pastor must be a large-souled man . . . large enough to take to his heart all classes of men . . . he stands especially near to the poor and despised. . . . He will have enemies to deal with as well as friends, and his heart must be large enough to love them all."

The pastor "must have a clear conviction that God has called him to this work. There should be no haste nor rashness in entering upon this office. In our Church there is none," he said, referring to the minister's "trial" period, course of study, and successive ordinations as deacon and elder. Bresee stated a final caution:

This is not a work of convenience to be taken up and laid down as we may or may not have other work to do. . . . A true condition of this work can only be drawn from the work of the

Son of God. We must stand in the shadow of the Cross . . . and as we gaze upon that dying Christ, and see the glory of the love of God in that marred face—waiting here, the true pastor learns the value of men . . . and feels that "'Tis all my business here below to cry, 'Behold the Lamb.'"

No other convention address approached Bresee's depth or oratorical power. One speaker was fearful of the "wrong class" of people streaming in from Europe, bringing "the superstition, ignorance and bigotry of the Scandinavians." Bresee was foremost in remembering the primitive Methodist vision of evangelism to the outcasts, learned in small Methodist churches in the Catskills.

Several Des Moines Annual Conference reports place Bresee in context. One, from 1876, urged that "all ministers set an example to the flock of deeper humility, greater freedom from worldly mindedness, and an entire consecration to the service of the Master . . . [and each] layman abstain from all sinful amusements [and] from an undue love of the world." Another is from 1878: "We rejoice that God is blessing this heritage with peace and prosperity, that the work of awakening conversion and sanctification is progressing among us." The third is Bishop Bowman's charge to ordinands in 1882: "The Bishop's address . . . consisted mainly in cautions respecting the doctrine of entire sanctification. . . . He especially urged the young men, and indeed the whole Conference, to be symmetrical in their preaching, not to be hobbyists. . . . he wanted to have the whole counsel of God declared, and not to have those who are monomaniacs on any point to control the policy of the Church."

Against this grid, where did Bresee stand in 1883? He took no exception to the first—he saw "worldliness" as a constant threat to ministers and laity. He probably agreed to the second, though he did not yet "speak plainly" about sanctification. About "hobbyists" and "monomaniacs," he probably agreed with Bishop Bowman, for Bresee was not yet active in the National Holiness Association, which had held camp meetings in Iowa but not in Bresee's conference. There is no evidence that he attended them or helped to organize the Iowa Holiness Association in 1879. Indeed, it is difficult to imagine him following Isaiah Reid, Iowa's holiness leader, who headed a "self-constituting presbytery" that ordained six holiness preachers at Centralia, Missouri, in 1883.

Methodism's uncertainty about the Holiness Movement was reflected in the conference paper. Shortly after Bishop Bowman's warning about "hobbyists" and "monomaniacs," it noted that the "*Guide to Holiness* is steadily increasing its circulation in all parts of the world." Bresee could not have been ignorant of the movement: it was too well known. There is potential evidence of Bresee's perfectionist views in his sermon manuscripts, but few can be dated with assurance to his Iowa days. One that is likely from the Iowa period was based on Ps. 84:5, "Blessed is the man whose strength is in thee." The theme was "The Blessedness of a Christian Life." It notes that Psalms portrays "a life of consecration to God . . . as not only wise but as eminently blessed," and that blessedness is "the divine source of the Christian's strength." The sermon specifically references Christian perfection: "We preach and believe in Christian perfection, but not that [it] precludes advancement. Man's immortal being is made for constant development and growth. Man's moral faculties and intellect never reach the highest of their power. Vast growth fits them for vaster development &c." This is Bresee's only sermon mentioning Christian perfection that seems definitely to be from Iowa, though there may be others. Bresee's sermons at this stage often emphasized moral development and spiritual growth.

Time to Move

Four of Bresee's associates reentered his life in California, including Osceola banker Henry Sigler and the "brilliant lawyer" from Clarinda, William McPherrin, who died of tuberculosis at Bresee's home. So did Nancy Radford, who met Bresee at Red Oak and, with her husband, followed him to Clarinda. In 1905, she joined Los Angeles First Church of the Nazarene and became an active deaconess there. Then there was H. D. Brown, who received his first preacher's license from Bresee. Brown became a pastor and presiding elder in South Dakota before moving to the Pacific Northwest. He was a presiding elder in Washington, pastor of Battery Street Methodist Episcopal Church in Seattle, and he organized a group out of which Seattle First Church of the Nazarene originated. He would become the first Nazarene district superintendent in 1904.

Bresee did not have to leave Iowa. He had conference responsibilities and enjoyed the trust of colleagues, bishops, and laity. Several churches "invited" him to be their pastor, hoping for the bishop's approval, but Bresee was determined to leave and considered an "invitation" from a Methodist church in San Antonio, where he had friends. But the South was not friendly toward a minister of Bresee's background and sympathies. He told Girvin that it was "sufficiently difficult to fight the world, the flesh, and the Devil, without also fighting prejudice," so he chose California instead.

Knotts had visited California and urged Bresee to consider it. Sigler was more influential. He had moved to Los Angeles and persuaded the presiding elder to invite Bresee to the conference. Such an invitation guaranteed a pastoral appointment.

Bresee sought advice from Bishop Simpson, who replied that southern California had a fine climate but little in the way of Methodist churches. The only strong one, he said, was Fort Street Church in Los Angeles. He judged it inopportune for Bresee to move. Bishop

John Hurst's knowledge of California was more current. Bresee wrote him also, offering to serve "any little church around the corner in Southern California." Hurst replied that he could have appointed Bresee to Oakland First had he known earlier of Bresee's interest. Bresee asked and received a letter of transfer from Bishop Simpson. Bishop Henry Warren received it, paving Bresee's way.

On Sunday, August 12, he addressed an audience at the Broadway Church. They departed five days later in a special car secured by a ticket agent in Omaha for the entourage. Ernest remained to study at Simpson College. The travel party included Bresee, who was forty-four, Maria, six of their children, Bresee's parents, and nephew Fred Cowley. Some friends also joined the party.

Their departure was noted by the Council Bluffs newspaper and by the Des Moines Annual Conference, which passed a resolution: "Resolved 1, That we deeply regret the departure of such an esteemed and valuable member of our Conference, one whose work in Iowa for 25 years has endeared him to many hearts and who has contributed so much to the growth of Iowa Methodism; Resolved 2, That we heartily recommend him to the esteem of our California brethren and trust that he may have the largest measure of success among them; Resolved 3, That should he hereafter desire to return to this Conference he will meet with a most cordial greeting."

PART THREE
CALIFORNIA

SEVEN

CALIFORNIA AND THE
RENEWAL OF MINISTRY

⌘

New York was the matrix of Bresee's early faith and call to ministry. He had matured as a pastor and administrator in Iowa. In California, he entered a new Methodist world where successes and failures brought unforeseen changes. Los Angeles had been founded by a Spanish governor and the priests of San Gabriel Mission. The United States seized it from Mexico in the 1840s. Railroads helped Americanize the region; the Southern Pacific Railroad came in 1876 and the Santa Fe in 1885. The population grew from eleven thousand to fifty thousand between 1880 and 1890.

The Bresees installed curtains and beds in their private railroad car, and a series of express and freight trains pulled them to Los Angeles via Sacramento. An immigrant's child died on the trip, and Bresee conducted a poignant funeral service beside the tracks. Their eight-day journey ended when Henry Sigler met them at the Southern Pacific depot and conducted them to a furnished house.

Sigler was now a real estate developer, but another Methodist family was better established in Los Angeles life: the extended Widney and Maclay family. The Widneys were Ohio folks who followed their mother's people west. Charles Maclay, their uncle, was a leading Santa Barbara citizen and state senator. Five Widney siblings settled in Los Angeles. The brothers became prominent businessmen. Their sister, Arabella, was prominent as well. They were unavoidable leaders in church and community, and Bresee encountered them immediately.

Robert Maclay Widney went west at sixteen, becoming a cattle driver, teamster, trapper, and hunter. He went to college in San Jose, earned a master's degree, and taught mathematics and other subjects. He studied law and was admitted to practice before the California and United States Supreme Courts. He entered real estate and published the *Real Estate Adventurer*. His newspaper and magazine articles ranged from money to religion. He became "Judge Widney" after a term on the Seventeenth Judicial District Court. He planned the University of Southern California, solicited its donors, led its Board of Directors upon its organization as a Methodist school in 1879, and gave one hundred thousand dollars to ensure its survival. He helped develop the harbor at San Pedro, fostered Santa Monica's development, invested in San Fernando, developed Long Beach, and was president of University Bank of Los Angeles. His loyalty to Los Angeles Methodism went back to its origins, when, as a class leader and Sunday school superintendent, he kept alive a struggling congregation without a pastor.

Joseph P. Widney remained in Ohio until he enlisted in the Civil War. He was assigned to hospital service on boats on the Ohio and Mississippi Rivers. He studied medicine in San Francisco and was an army physician in Arizona during a campaign against the Apaches. In 1868 he entered private practice in Los Angeles, serving Anglos and Hispanics. He was founder and president of the Los Angeles County Medical Society and a member of the state board of health. He led the Los Angeles Board of Education. He drew up plans with Robert for San Pedro harbor, donated land to the University of Southern California, and served on its first board of trustees. He joined Robert and A. M. Hough, Bresee's boyhood pastor in Davenport, on the university's endowment board. The J. P. Widneys, Arabella, and their aunt Eleanor Maclay were members of Fort Street Methodist Episcopal Church in 1883, when Bresee arrived.

There were other Methodist leaders. Sigler belonged to University Methodist Episcopal Church, was president of the State Sunday School Association, and promoted camp meetings and real estate development in Long Beach as a member of the Southern California Conference's Seaside Resort Committee. A. M. Hough was University Church's founding pastor. In 1864, he left New York for the rowdy mining town of Virginia City, Montana, where he started a church. He was armed with a heavy revolver when he first arrived in Los Angeles. Presiding elder R. W. C. Farnsworth edited the *Southern California Methodist Quarterly*. A graduate of Wesleyan University, he supported revivals and sanctification. Marion McKinley Bovard, university president, was from a distinguished family of ministers. Hough, Bovard, and the Widneys were close, and Bresee entered into their circle. E. S. Chase, "an old style preacher" who struck "a strong note of evangelism," was skilled in organization, fund-raising, and business.

The day after arriving in Los Angeles, the Bresees attended Fort Street Methodist Episcopal Church, southern California's oldest and largest Methodist congregation. Chase ushered Bresee to the pulpit and had him preach. The next Sunday, Bresee preached for Hough at University Church. The annual conference convened that next week at Fort Street. There were fifty-two ministers and four districts. Bishop Henry Warren received Bresee's transfer on the first day and welcomed him to the conference.

The significance of a minor conference action no doubt escaped Bresee: B. A. Washburn's case was referred to an investigating committee. Bishop Warren announced later that Washburn "had surrendered his parchments." The conference also "voted to commit one of the parchments surrendered by Hardin Wallace to the care of Bishop Warren." A report alluded to these cases: "Resolved, that no member of this Conference shall employ any evangelist or any person doing the work of an evangelist on his charge, unless such evangelist or person shall have an annual written certificate of character and fitness for evangelistic work from the Presiding Elder." Wallace, once a pastor and presiding elder in Illinois, became an evangelist in 1872. In 1877, he spurred the organization of a holiness association in east Texas. In California, he conducted a notable revival at Fort Street Church in 1881. His followers were gathering into bands under the name of the Southern California and Arizona Holiness Association. Bresee joined the conference just as tensions were developing over entire sanctification and independent evangelists. He probably had no inkling of his future role in these matters.

Bresee was appointed examiner for third-year candidates in the course of study, conference visitor to the University of Southern California, preacher of the annual missionary sermon, and pastor of the Fort Street Church. He had landed safely on California's shores.

Fort Street Methodist Episcopal Church

Fort Street Church, organized in 1867, was the largest of the district's thirty-nine churches. It fostered University Church under Bovard's guidance and spawned Asbury Church, dedicated debt-free by J. P. Widney. There was Sunday worship, class meeting on Tuesday evening, and prayer meeting on Thursday. Chase enlarged the building, added a balcony, installed an organ, and introduced the practice of decorating the pulpit with flowers. The practice continued under Bresee; the whole platform was embellished on Easter. The Bresees occupied an adjacent parsonage. These boom years for both city and church saw membership rise from 437 to 650.

Soon after arriving, Bresee dedicated a new church in Pomona and "managed the finances," a primary goal at every dedication, calling for seven hundred dollars to erase the debt. The crowd gave $833. He dedicated Grace Methodist Episcopal Church in December. "The sermon, a very elevating one, was preached by Rev. Bro. Bresee from Isaiah xl: 9, 10." A district convention in December explored many topics. A reporter noted, "On the subject of 'Christian Holiness,' Rev. P. F. Bresee preached a powerful and convincing sermon." In February 1884, the Los Angeles Medical Society met with civic leaders, including the governor, mayor, university president, and clergy. The California *Christian Advocate* reported that "Science and Religion received a short and good speech from Rev. P. F. Bresee." That fall Bresee led a "delightful and well-attended Thanksgiving" service at Fort Street. He spoke at a children's meeting in Pasadena. He served on the Seaside Resort Committee, delivering "a very able and interesting oration" on Washington and Lincoln, dedicated a church in San Fernando, and conducted a "home camp-meeting" at Fort Street. He lectured in Santa Ana, preached the missionary sermon at annual conference, welcomed Monday morning preachers' meetings in his study, conducted a memorial service for Bishop Simpson, and hosted the 1884 annual conference. All this was during Bresee's first fifteen months in Los Angeles. In addition, he returned to Iowa in June 1884 to receive the honorary doctor of divinity degree from Simpson Centenary College.

Farnsworth's next annual conference report shows that Bresee was exercising his many gifts in California. Farnsworth called Fort Street

> the largest and most completely equipped church in the Conference. It has a host of devout members, a large number of busy workers, and reaches the people through a variety of religious efforts. The prayer and class meetings are largely attended, and

are full of spiritual life and unction. The crowded attendance at preaching and Sunday school continues undiminished. . . . this large, influential and representative church—one which is in many respects the mother of our churches in Southern California—is a truly pious and working church, and has the pure Gospel ably and boldly preached from its pulpit every Sabbath.

A district convention in late 1883 responded to attacks from the independent holiness bands and promoted the theology and experience of entire sanctification in the very churches that Wallace and Washburn's followers were criticizing. A writer viewed the problem:

California has been afflicted with a peculiar phase of the "holiness" movement. A set of men cutting loose from all Church responsibility have organized themselves into a "band," and travel all over the State, holding their meetings. . . . [They] built up a sort of scriptural aristocracy. They look down with pity, if not contempt, on all who do not profess as they do. They are constantly making flings at "Churchianity."

Bresee replied for the Methodist ministers with great clarity. His text was Ps. 51:10: "Create in me a clean heart, O God." Methodism, he said, did not begin in doctrinal controversy. It was more practical than doctrinal, insisting on life rather than dogma. The General Rules of the Methodist societies required only one condition: a desire to flee the wrath to come and be saved from sin. Methodism, Bresee said, teaches the promises of God with their privileges and blessings. The chief Methodist doctrines are "the fatherhood of God, the Deity of Jesus Christ, the presence and power and divinity of the Holy Ghost, [and] His influence upon the human heart, preparing and enabling the Christian man to grow in grace." Within this scope comes the cry for a clean heart. The psalmist was awakened from the absolute death of sin; this conversion should not be taken lightly. Repentance includes hatred for sin, seeking after righteousness, and total consecration to God. A "born again" person experiences a resurrection, or, like Elijah, a "translation," and is entirely given up to God and has the fruit of the Spirit. But is that person wholly sanctified? "It seems to me to be the teaching of the word, and of Christian experience that men are not usually wholly sanctified at conversion." It is too early to say that the "last remains of the carnal mind are destroyed." When we find any evil way in us, we are to "drag it forth—bring it into the light of God's face . . . feel the blood passing over the corruption of our nature."

Is this a growth or an instantaneous work? "The death of sin is never a growth." But there is more: weeds are not removed just to remove weeds but so that flowers and fruit can grow unobstructed. "Holiness is no more an end—it is that the graces of the Spirit may live and grow in us." "I plead for a holiness worthy of our religion," said Bresee. A humble testimony is blessed; grander still is a life that speaks of this glorious transformation of character. Bresee referenced those holiness people who would "create schism in the Church of God . . . [make holiness] a pretense for slandering the ministers of religion, and slighting the means of grace . . . [and] forsake the mother that bore them and turn their back on the churches that have carried them in their arms." Bresee insisted: "Let the testimony we give to all men of our piety be the love we bear to all men."

The Methodist ministers responded to Bresee's message with resolutions. First, they said, "it is the recognized duty of Methodist preachers to preach and teach this blessed doctrine of holiness and perfect love . . . and that our people be still urged to seek and obtain a clean heart and all the fullness of God, and that the ordinary and extraordinary means of grace be used for this end." They authorized a committee with Farnsworth, Chase, Bresee, and Leslie F. Gay to approach the National Holiness Association about forming a California branch. Further, they asked the committee to consider forming holiness bands "whose work shall be to go into unoccupied fields, or to the help of such pastors as may need or desire their assistance." A final resolution deplored, "with great sorrow," the "part of some calling themselves 'The Holy People'. . . to create schism in the Church of God." So the convention affirmed "scriptural holiness," affirmed the National Holiness Association, and encouraged "Holiness bands" that served the church, not split it.

The Annual Conference of 1884

Bresee hosted the 1884 annual conference at Fort Street. Church membership had risen to 501, the pastor's salary to $2,315. Bresee joined the Board of Church Extension and continued as a University of Southern California director. He became examiner of students in the course of study's fourth year, preached the missionary sermon, and sat on various committees, including one to draw up the conference's new permanent rules of order.

Northern California Methodists had adopted resolutions on sanctification and the holiness bands, and Bovard asked the Southern California Conference to accept them too. A document lays out the grounds of dispute. Ministers and people, it says, were faithful to the doctrinal standards on "Christian Perfection." John Wesley, John Fletcher, and Richard Watson were "accepted authorities." "We cannot take any lower ground than that sin in believers may be and ought to be, extirpated by God, the Spirit, through faith in our Lord Jesus Christ. . . . Perfect love is a privilege and grace attainable by faith, and our pastors should be examples and teachers in this as in all things." But the Union Holiness Bands were sharply criticized. Their leaders were termed "irresponsible, insubordinate, erratic and fanatical, who reject the advice and control of pastors and official boards, and set themselves forth as the special exponents and exemplars of holiness."

"A few of our people," it continued, are "exhausting their energies and resources in work alien to our own institutions and agencies." The document approved the policy of the National Holiness Association, which worked harmoniously with pastors. Ministers and official boards were not to lend their churches to the separatists. "The best methods of promoting Christian perfection" were Bible study, reading about sanctified Christians, preaching "the whole truth," attending the means of grace, supporting church institutions, secret prayer, and "direct seeking for perfect love with implicit trust in God." The document illustrates how the broader Holiness Movement was divided between NHA "loyalists" and "come-outers." California Methodism was forming an alliance with the NHA. Farnsworth's report on the Los Angeles District underscored the prevailing current of religious revival: "A general revival spirit with occasional conversions has pervaded the University Church and the College much of the year. . . . Special holiness meetings have been held weekly in Fort Street, Grace, and University Churches."

The *Quarterly* and Holiness Evangelism

The plan to work with the NHA bore fruit in early 1885 in the coming of "those world-renowned, matchless, Methodist loyalists and Holiness exponents," Rev. William McDonald of Boston and Rev. Geo. D. Watson from Florida. McDonald had pastored numerous churches and had promoted holiness revivals with John Inskip and J. A. Wood in America, England, Italy, and India. The NHA president, McDonald edited *The Christian Witness and Advocate of Bible Holiness.* Watson was an NHA vice president.

In March the *Southern California Methodist Quarterly* reported glowingly on three weeks of meetings at Bresee's church and published an abridged version of McDonald's sermon on "Sanctification Wholly." Farnsworth, the *Quarterly*'s editor, recommended the

Christian Witness, adding: "The old prophets, Christ, Paul, Wesley, Edwards, Moody, and most great preachers who have left their impress upon the Church, believed in special revivals and special efforts for such. Can we ordinary men improve on their methods?" The *Quarterly* reflected the ethical concern of the Methodist holiness people. Farnsworth pushed temperance reform, while Arabella Widney wrote about "Church Entertainments," warning against raising money through entertainments that do not command respect or reverence for the place where they are given. The church's social life should lead to prayerful spiritual benefit, she argued. The *Quarterly* extensively covered a five-day convention, a seven-day camp meeting, and a four-day Chautauqua Assembly at the Long Beach Methodist campground in August 1885. Bresee's Children's Day presentation was summarized:

> [Children] are all members of the church, especially the baptized children, and they are the soul of the church. They have not taken their own vow yet, but their parents have assumed the responsibility for them. They are to be taught and led . . . from the very earliest moment. If we keep emphasizing the salvation of their souls, they will get saved. Boys and girls hunger to become members of the church. It leads them more to believe on the Lord Jesus Christ. Children should be brought to preaching services and put under its holy influences. Get the children before the devil gets a mortgage on them.

The next afternoon, Leslie F. Gay gave an extended Bible reading on "Holiness." Fifteen persons at the altar "expressed a desire to be sanctified wholly." Bresee preached that evening. Bresee preached again on the camp meeting's final evening, insisting that "if the M.E. Church was consecrated to God, as it ought to be, it would be strong enough to take the world for Christ." A notable scene followed: "At the close of the preaching service, those that received a clean heart during the camp meeting, were invited to the altar. A few moments were spent in testimony, after which parting songs were sung, and songs pledging our fidelity to God."

The conference's 1885 Report on the State of the Church rejoiced "that the Church still holds with a firm grasp the doctrine of perfect love, and that it is preached from the pulpits as the blessed privilege of all God's people." Presiding elders spoke to the issue. Farnsworth reported "unusual revival efforts" around Los Angeles, noting that "a great number of Christians have found a better experience." John Green, Fresno District, stated: "We were apprehensive a year ago that there would be serious defection in some of our charges, on the subject of Christian perfection . . . But the preachers, as far as I know, have been . . . zealous in teaching this great truth, and most of the members have been loyal and consistent." Farnsworth gave such witness again in 1886 and 1887, but the conference was turning its attention to other matters, evidently feeling that it had warded off the holiness raiders. The 1888 minutes reflect no concern about scriptural holiness. Farnsworth had died the preceding January.

Bresee's memories offer a somewhat different account of his three years in Los Angeles. Looking back, he saw himself influenced by some "fully sanctified" members but not yet completely one with them in spirit. "They were clear, sound, substantial, evangelical." They "earnestly and intelligently," but quietly, pushed "the work of full salvation." He saw himself assisting them in holiness work. They, in turn, prayed "for him" but not "at him" and supported his ministry. "The spiritual life of the church continually increased, and there was a good degree of blessing on my ministry, the church rapidly growing in every way." The group included Leslie Gay, Clarence McKee, Dr. Michael Everley Whisler, and Mrs. Griggs. Their interest in "full salvation" predated Hardin Wallace's 1881 revival at Fort Street Church but was reinforced by that event. Bresee said that he was "in general accord with both the teaching and the spirit of the brethren" but had no special consciousness of his own "lack and need."

"An Indescribable Ball of Condensed Light"

Soon, however, Bresee awakened to "the deep necessities" of his own heart. "This realization grew more and more intense until my heart cry began to go out to God for the mighty grace that was adequate to all my needs." At this time, presumably during his second year at Fort Street, he experienced a new spiritual awareness. Its only evidence is Bresee's personal account given by Girvin, who places the account in quotation marks, indicating that—as a professional court recorder—he recorded Bresee's words verbatim.

At this time there came to me in answer to prayer, a very striking experience. I had been for some time in almost constant prayer, and crying to God for something that would meet my needs, not clearly realizing what they were or how they could be met. I sat alone in the parsonage, in the cool of evening, in the front parlor near the door. The door being opened, I looked up in the azure in earnest prayer, while the shades of evening gathered about. As I waited and waited, and continued in prayer, looking up, it seemed to me as if from the azure there came a meteor, an indescribable ball of condensed light, descending rapidly toward me. As I gazed upon it, it was soon within a few score feet, when I seemed distinctly to hear a voice saying, as my face was upturned towards it: "Swallow it; swallow it," and in an instant it fell upon my lips and face. I attempted to obey the injunction. It seemed to me, however, that I swallowed only a little of it, although it felt like fire upon my lips, and the burning sensation did not leave them for several days. While all of this of itself would be nothing, there came with it into my heart and being, a transformed condition of life and blessing and unction and glory, which I had never known before. I felt that my need was supplied. I was always very reticent in reference to my own personal experience. I have never gotten over it, and I have said very little relative to this; but there came into my ministry a new element of spiritual life and power. People began to come into the blessing of full salvation; there were more persons converted; and the last year of my ministry in that church was more consecutively successful, being crowned by an almost constant revival. When the third year came to a close, the church had been nearly doubled in membership, and in every way built up.

Some have considered this Bresee's "crisis experience" of entire sanctification. The "ball of condensed light" is regarded variously as a literal miraculous work of the Holy Spirit, an allegorical expression of a spiritual reality, or a mystical experience. Close examination, though, makes these interpretations difficult to sustain.

First, some items are precise and literal. Bresee was alone, in the front parlor, near the open door. The sky was blue, the temperature was falling, and evening gave way to night. The "meteor" is not defined but is described precisely: "an indescribable ball of condensed light" descending rapidly. It came "a few score feet" from him. His face was "upturned." The light touched his lips and face. He tried to "swallow it" but swallowed "only a little of it." It left a burning sensation on his lips that lasted several days.

Second, Bresee's words contain speech that is indirect, allegorical, or allusive. "It seemed to me as if" in reference to the "meteor." It was "indescribable." "I seemed distinctly to hear a voice." The command, "Swallow it; swallow it," spoken twice, reminds one of Augustine hearing a voice say: "Take up and read; take up and read." Then "it seemed" that he swallowed only "a little of it." And yet, more literally, "it felt like fire on my lips." Bresee's account somewhat parallels Ezekiel, where a "likeness" of a human form is encircled by brightness, "the appearance of fire," who commands Ezekiel to eat a scroll. It is as "sweet as honey" to Ezekiel's lips. Another possibility is Isa. 6:6-7, but there the lips are touched but the fire is not swallowed. Bresee's story remains obscure; there may be no scriptural allusion at all. Bresee may have tried to be literal, but he qualifies it with "it seemed."

Third, the religious meaning was more important than the physical phenomenon. The "meteor" in itself would have been nothing, he says. What accompanied it was significant: "a transformed condition of life and blessing and unction and glory" and "a new element of spiritual life and power" in his ministry. Bresee was no gullible miracle mongerer. He does not describe this experience as the second blessing, purity of heart, entire sanctification, or perfect love. He simply says "my need was supplied" and "I have never gotten over it." He did not regard it as his "entire sanctification," for he never repudiated his testimony about sanctification during his Chariton pastorate. Further, Bresee told Girvin that he was "always reticent" to refer to his own religious experience, and Bresee's writings never reference the "meteor." For him, religious experience was validated by effective ministry—people coming "into the blessing of full salvation," more converts, the church doubled in membership "and in every way built up."

The "ball of condensed light" may have been "ball lightning" or "globe lightning," which can die silently or explosively, often hisses, and may leave a distinct odor. It usually occurs during atmospheric electrical discharges, which is not incompatible with the "azure" sky. Science offers no agreed explanation of the phenomenon. The detail of the open door coincides with this possibility, and Bresee may have heard hissing that "seemed" to say, "Swallow it, swallow it." He was sure that he had experienced something physical. There is no need to invoke miracle or mysticism here. For Bresee, the unusual was unnecessary. The physical phenomenon was not important in itself. The significant thing was the spiritual awareness that occurred—"unction" or even "a mighty baptism with the Holy Ghost."

Whatever Bresee's later memories, Methodist sources support the conclusion that by calling upon Holiness Movement leaders to promote Wesleyan teaching, Bresee came either to a personal deepening or to a reappropriation of his Iowa experience.

Leaving Fort Street

Bresee chaired a session of the 1886 annual conference in the bishop's absence. The conference put Bresee on the Long Beach Resort Association board. Unusual growth had marked his Fort Street ministry. Los Angeles's population had surged soon after he arrived, and his labors matched the challenge. The Thursday prayer meetings often attracted four hundred to five hundred people. A congregational historian observed: "Financial prosperity attended the church, all debts were paid, and material improvements implemented. The church will never recover from the spiritual shock he gave it but under its impulse will go on to all eternity, adding stars to the Redeemer's crown." Bresee was satisfied with his ministry there. He enjoyed near unanimous support but said: "I did not preach the second work of grace very definitely. I preached it, but did not give it such emphasis." Then he added: "If I had known more when I came to this coast, and had had experience and sense, I could have swept the whole of Methodism into holiness."

He received into church membership his parents, wife, and the children: Ernest, Phineas, Bertha, and Paul; also Fred Cowley, his nephew. Melvin and Susan became probationary members in August 1885. For once the entire family belonged to the same congregation; it never happened again.

Bresee moved on, but Fort Street remained the church of J. P. Widney, his brothers Samuel and William, Arabella, and Judge Widney's children. Judge Widney, though, belonged to University Church. During these years, J. P. Widney proposed a school of medicine for the university, launched it as its first dean, and donated land and buildings to make it possible. Widney's uncle, Senator Charles Maclay, had come to California as a Methodist home missionary. The senator gave land and resources to establish Maclay School of Theology at San Fernando. Robert Maclay, his brother, became dean. Bresee was later a trustee of this institution.

Some Fort Street members later became Nazarenes, including Bresee's mother, wife, Melvin, Susan, Dr. and Mrs. Joseph Widney, and Arabella Widney. And there were the McKees, the Fred Howlands, Alice P. Baldwin, Valentine Jacques, E. G. Hauxhurst and family, and the prime mover in holiness revivalism at Fort Street— Leslie F. Gay. Fort Street proved the seedbed of a new denomination.

EIGHT

PASADENA

⟋⟍

Bishop Henry Warren appointed Bresee to Pasadena First Methodist Episcopal Church in 1886. He also became a director of the Chautauqua Assembly. The Chautauqua movement was replacing camp meetings, substituting Christian education for the camp meeting's spiritual program. In annual conference business, Bresee joined Bovard in presenting a resolution "to smite the liquor traffic." Farnsworth emphasized Bresee's work at Fort Street in the district report:

There has been an increased effort to save the people. This has been along the various lines of prayer-meetings, class-meetings, children's classes, camp-meetings, special revival efforts, and the preaching of a fervent gospel in the regular ministrations. This salvation has been in all the fullness and richness of old-time Methodism. . . . The [prayer meeting] at Fort Street has regularly a full house and a saving power.

Bresee followed A. W. Bunker at Pasadena. The church had 142 members. If Fort Street Church was the seedbed of a new denomination, Pasadena First Church was Bresee's laboratory. Pasadena First was Bresee's longest Methodist pastorate, and records from those years are remarkably complete. A congregational historian noted that 1886 to 1888 was "the most dramatic period of our history" due to the southern California land boom. In 1870 one of Judge Robert Widney's companies marketed portions of the San Pasqual Plantation, an old Spanish land grant. In 1874 an Indiana land company bought twenty-eight hundred acres and sold lots to Hoosiers, who colonized the area and organized Pasadena. The Hoosiers worshiped in homes until a union Sunday school opened. A Methodist class was organized in 1876, and A. M. Hough dedicated the first building, which seated two hundred. It was later moved on rollers to the town's emerging center.

The land boom was underway when Bresee arrived, and Methodists were constructing a larger building at Colorado Street and Marengo Avenue. Bresee and Bovard had delivered the primary speeches when the cornerstone was laid back in April. Now, in September, the Bresees moved to Pasadena, occupying a new parsonage east of the church. The family, though, was scattering: Phineas W. remained in Los Angeles, and Fred Cowley lived in San Diego.

Bresee promised to "make a fire that would reach heaven" and began a protracted meeting in the old building. He and coworkers sang hymns at the intersection of Colorado and Fair Oaks, gathered a crowd of men, knelt to pray, invited the crowd to the meeting, sang another hymn, and led a procession to the little church one block west. He reported forty conversions; only one was a woman. The men were evidently new arrivals, without their families, seeking work. The church's remarkable growth was underway. Class meetings were well attended. New members were added. Bresee lectured to the Young Men's Christian Association and participated with Hough, Judge Widney, and Farnsworth in laying the cornerstone for the Maclay School of Theology at San Fernando. The church began meeting in the new building amid ongoing construction. In February Bresee hosted a temperance rally at which five hundred people signed an anti-saloon petition.

Bishop Fowler spoke at the church dedication on March 20. The newspaper described the church as sixty-eight by seventy-six feet, divided into an auditorium, classrooms, a chapel, and a ladies' parlor equipped with kitchen and stove. Evidently it was built on the "Akron Plan," with a balcony around the auditorium. Classrooms under the balcony had sliding doors that opened onto the auditorium. The windows were stained glass. Vestibules under the 150-foot tower opened onto both streets. "All the floors are to be covered with Brussels carpet."

It was the height of middle-class fashion, yet Bresee was losing interest. He had not forgotten those men on the street corner, or his longing for the great revival fire that would reach heaven. He pressed the claims of the gospel in the new building and at May's quarterly conference reported 146 new members and 24 new probationers. Prayer meetings thrived and new classes were organized. Bresee conducted a Decoration Day service in the new sanctuary, dispensing "a patriotic discourse." In June he preached on "The Law of the Reproduction of Spiritual Forces" and "Some of the Mistakes of Moses, and Some Things That Were Not Mistakes." There were converts and new members, many by transfer.

In July Bresee reported 197 new members by letter, 14 moved from probationary to full membership, and 34 probationers. Only 14 members had been lost. Sunday school attendance averaged 300. There were seventeen Methodist classes, including a pastor's class for young men. Ten new class leaders had been appointed. Children's work was growing. The quarterly conference unanimously recommended Bresee's return for another year.

He could have been satisfied. He was not. He rejoiced in the "general prosperity" and "growing spirituality" but harbored misgivings. "I am sadly conscious," he said, "of the need of much greater spiritual power in the church." Bresee sensed that the prosperity and respectability evident in the new building could distract from evangelism. And there was his growing conviction that the building was too full and more space was already needed.

Bishop Walden convened the 1887 annual conference at Fort Street. The election of delegates to the 1888 General Conference showed the broad acceptability of the holiness stalwarts: Farnsworth was elected a clergy delegate on the first ballot, and Leslie F. Gay was elected a lay alternate. Farnsworth's final report as Bresee's presiding elder reported four hundred conversions on the district that year. His final words were: "May the Holy Spirit's baptism so rest upon us as to keep us saved, faithful, and victorious in these days of our opportunity and responsibility." Bresee was losing an ally on the cabinet of presiding elders but could rejoice that Farnsworth was the new dean of the Maclay theological seminary.

Bishop Walden sent Bresee back to Pasadena, and the official board raised his salary to three thousand dollars. In October the official board considered proposals to enlarge the new church, add an auditorium to the south, or build outlying churches. Bresee reported continuing membership growth and stressed that larger facilities were needed. A proposal to build a tabernacle on Marengo Avenue was approved.

Late in 1887, a concert was given by Philip Phillips, the gospel songwriter. The concert netted $260, which was put at Bresee's disposal "for the relief of the poor." The church organist was given a volume of Longfellow's poems—perhaps her only compensation; in his Nazarene years, Bresee opposed paying musicians, lest they become mere entertainers.

In 1887 Bresee instituted a Christmas love feast, drawing upon the love feasts that John Wesley had learned from the Moravians. The love feast was marked by sharing bread and water and Christian testimony. Bresee recounted the event: "I felt strangely impelled to announce and hold a love feast. On Christmas morning, to the surprise of everybody, the house was filled with people. Already in this church the holiness work had become predominant, and this meeting was a gathering to some extent of the holiness forces of Southern California." On this Christmas Day, Rev. J. N. Marsh's wife "arose in the middle of the church and stood and testified and praised God with outstretched hands and burning hallelujahs." Bresee said: "The outpouring of the Holy Spirit was so great and mighty, that probably it had never been equaled in the church in Southern California up to that time." The love feast was a means for expressing Wesley's "perfect love," and it became a gathering of the Holiness Movement.

The Two Tabernacles

In January 1888, Bresee reported 206 new members and 55 new probationary members. By July there were 620 members "in full connection," of whom 257 had been received since January 1. The quarterly conference, by a standing vote, requested Bresee's appointment for another year. Bresee also reported seventy-two members dismissed by letter; they had moved away, for Pasadena was in flux. Bresee favored constructing a large auditorium south of the new church to accommodate the crowds, which he expected to grow, but the quarterly conference postponed a decision. The official board met on February 27 to consider the tabernacle proposal, but opposition surfaced in a motion by assistant pastor James Miller, a retired part-time minister. Other alternatives were explored in following months, but the church returned to Bresee's view in April, and construction proceeded.

The building was known as the Methodist Tabernacle. A large, barnlike structure, its front corners were "churchly" but unstylish towers, with a large entrance between them. The inside was plain, lacking frescos or stained glass, with neat borders and designs on the walls and some carpeting in the aisles. The platform arrangement resembled the church next door, but everything was larger. A fine curved Communion rail, supported by more than fifty turned posts paralleled the rounded platform. The choir sat facing the congregation. A piano or organ was off to one side. On the floor there were individual chairs in neat rows. Balconies were on three sides. The tabernacle cost $10,700 and seated two thousand people. It was used on Sunday mornings and for other large meetings. It also became, in effect, Pasadena's town hall and was used until 1900, when it and the church were razed. The tabernacle was first put to use on the first Sunday in August, with visiting ministers and "a grand chorus choir," but Bresee was absent due to sickness. He did not preach in it until late September.

Around the move into the tabernacle, Bresee called the church board to a special meeting chaired by the assistant minister. Bresee was absent, but there were two eminent visitors: Judge Robert Widney and presiding elder G. F. Bovard, brother of university president M. M. Bovard. Something was afoot. The minutes state that Widney asked "this Official Board that we consent to the release of Dr. Bresee as our Pastor for the next conference year in order to open the way to his appointment as pastor of Simpson Church." The judge "recited the facts" about the Simpson Church, answered questions, and then left.

The official board already knew about the Simpson Church. Judge Widney had published an account of its origins in the *Southern California Christian Advocate*. The *Los Angeles Times* had reprinted it. Los Angeles had spread south and west of Fort Street Church, and a church was needed in the new residential area. Bresee first told Widney the proposal, and Bresee arranged meetings between Widney, Bishop Warren, Farnsworth, Hough, and others. The bishop appointed Judge Widney to a committee to secure a lot, and one was purchased in late 1886. Bresee had been involved in the project from the beginning; he may have been its instigator. His hand appears in Simpson's organization and name. Like Simpson Centenary College, the church was named for Bishop Matthew Simpson. "Tabernacle" was another of Bresee's favorite words. E. W. Caswell became its pastor in September, and construction began in December. Judge Widney's visit to Pasadena was to secure Bresee as Caswell's immediate successor who would complete the construction and nurture the church. Bresee's early dreams for Simpson Tabernacle were being realized. Judge Widney was Sunday school superintendent and president of the Board of Trustees. Phineas W. Bresee was on the Board of Stewards. Bresee's old New York pastor, Hough, was a class leader. Bresee might well consider leading a church of his own planning with the support of family and friends.

Simpson Church's scale is gleaned from descriptions of the completed tabernacle in 1891. The building used about 1.25 million bricks. A report on the interior states:

> Seated with Opera and Movable Chairs. Seating capacity, 2,500. Lighted by Gas and Electricity. Ventilated and heated by outside air conducted in pipes to the furnace room and thence distributed underneath the floor to registers, one of which placed underneath each chair, thus giving fresh air and even temperature to all parts of the room and no perceptible draft. The acoustic properties of the auditorium are probably the most perfect in the United States, while the musical effect of its resonance is marvelous.

Caught between two tabernacles of his own planning, Bresee could feel some obligation to serve either one. Pasadena's plain tabernacle was in use. Simpson's magnificent tabernacle was still unfinished. Neither was paid for.

Pasadena First Church's official board decided: "We do not deem it expedient to consent to the withdrawal of Dr. Bresee from the pastorate of this church." The matter was ended. Another pastor went to

Simpson, and then another. The building was in use a year before its completion in November 1890. It was extravagantly praised. Bishop Fowler said, "I have been in every auditorium worthy of the name in America and Europe, and I do not hesitate to say this is the best I have ever seen." It was the second largest auditorium in southern California and the largest church building on the Pacific Coast. Bresee did not abandon his vision, though, nor was he through with Simpson Tabernacle.

The pastoral address at the 1889 annual conference picked up the theme of worldliness: "The Methodist Episcopal Church takes high Scriptural grounds against card-playing, theater-going, wine-drinking, and other social customs and amusements condemned by God's word." It did not specify tobacco, but many Methodists opposed its use.

How to Abound, How to Be Abased

In his first two years in Pasadena, the population grew from under two thousand to around fifteen thousand, and Bresee had learned how to "abound" (Phil. 4:12). Then land prices collapsed, and he, the city, and the church had to learn to be abased.

Pasadena's boom was followed by a bust. By late 1886, there were fifty-three active real estate agencies. Restaurants fed a thousand customers daily, and land sales had totaled five million dollars. People flocked to Pasadena, bringing money. Parading brass bands led them to land auctions. There were solid gains: homes were built and commercial property was developed. Then land values collapsed suddenly. A lot on Colorado Street that sold for $150 before the boom jumped quickly to $8,000, and then fell back to its original value. One man invested a respectable fortune, lost it, and ended up as a menial laborer on a chicken farm.

At annual conference in September 1888, presiding elder G. F. Bovard admitted that "it is universally conceded that this has been the hardest year financially that we have seen for some time." He mentioned the decision to build the Pasadena tabernacle, though noting "differences of opinion" regarding it. The Pasadena Sunday school, however, could "justly pride herself in having the largest average attendance within the bounds of the Conference, if not of Methodism on the Pacific coast."

Bresee, however, faced a financial crisis. The church was in arrears on the salaries of the pastor, assistant pastor, and janitor. The board ordered them paid in full, and formed a committee to "apportion the expenses on the members." Bresee's salary was set at three thousand dollars for the next year. Miller was rehired for only six months at a lower salary. In October, Bresee's salary was raised, and he was granted a five-week vacation. In November, the Bresees were honored with a Thanksgiving Day reception.

There was a notable funeral in January. Owen Brown, one of fiery abolitionist John Brown's sons, was the last survivor of his father's famous attack on Harper's Ferry. He homesteaded a claim in the mountains. He died on January 8, and his funeral was held in the tabernacle. Bresee co-officiated.

Bresee's report in January began well: "I am thankful that my health has been so largely restored. I think that at no time during my connection with the church has the spiritual life been so deep and earnest as at present. A goodly number have been converted and many have gone on to higher attainments. The baptized children's class is doing good work." The next section reflected a church and pastor who were "learning to be abased": "The great depression [is] driving many people from the city to seek employment [and reducing] the ability of our people to contribute, multiplying the cases among us of absolute need to prevent actual suffering in our midst." There was also membership loss to new Methodist churches started at Monk Hill and Olivewood.

Miller resigned as assistant pastor in March. The board expressed regret that "financial stringency" made this necessary. By April membership was down to 536 but Sunday school attendance was at 350. The board voted to seek "the most favorable assessment possible" from the tax assessor.

Quarterly conference minutes from July 1 show the trend. The church had 142 full and probationary members when Bresee arrived. It had received 962 new members, for a total of 1,104. But 510 members had left "in various ways," leaving 594. Of these, 526 were full members; the rest were on probation. The downward trend had continued that quarter: 45 new full and probationary members, but 53 people had transferred out.

Bovard asked about pastoral supply for the coming year. A resolution was offered commending Bresee's "untiring zeal," the "fearlessness, the wisdom, and the vigor of his pulpit utterances upon questions of public policy," and his guidance "through a period of unprecedented prosperity" and now "in this time of financial depression." It was adopted unanimously, asking Bovard to convey to the cabinet their desire for Bresee's return.

Pasadena had other Methodist churches. There was a congregation of about seventy-five "colored members" who worshiped in the old city hall, and a congregation of the Methodist Episcopal Church, South, which had no church building but had some substantial city leaders. Under Bresee, Pasadena First Church began sponsoring a Chinese mission. In 1887, a similar work had begun at Los Angeles Fort Street Church and then spread. A photograph of the Pasadena congregation shows twenty-two persons, mostly in Chinese attire.

First Church business meetings that summer and fall dealt repeatedly with finances. Bresee reported membership losses in November but also "rich baptisms of the Spirit, some souls seeking and finding the highway of holiness, and a few have been converted." The next month, there was this newspaper advertisement:

There will be held a Christmas love-feast at the M.E. Church on Christmas Day, beginning at 9 a.m. A general invitation is extended to all who would like to enjoy such a service, to attend. There was a great meeting of this kind last year, the memory of which is fragrant with all those who had the privilege of being present. This year we would make the feast as wide as possible. "Whosoever will let him come and partake of the water of life freely." P. F. Bresee, Pastor.

This was a holiness rally—the likely meaning behind "general invitation" and "feast as wide as possible." This "moveable feast" would follow Bresee from place to place and into the Church of the Nazarene.

By 1890, Pasadena's decline was turning. Bresee belonged to the Bankers' Alliance and reported at First Church's quarterly conference in February that there was "prosperity in all particulars." The church received fifty-eight members, only twelve were dismissed, and "a goodly number have been converted, and some have entered into the richer experience of entire sanctification." The May and August reports showed losses, continuing financial problems, but greater organization for coping

Preaching Holiness

Holiness was a central theme in Bresee's ministry from the Fort Street years on, but more persistently in Pasadena. His public statements show a steady progression of candor. He also told Girvin about "a number of special meetings . . . conducted by the holiness evangelists, William McDonald, J. A. Wood, and others."

Who were these evangelists? William McDonald, a National Holiness Association founder, was a "Methodist loyalist." John Allen

Wood was another NHA founder who had served Methodist pastorates in New York and Pennsylvania. Wood professed entire sanctification at a camp meeting in 1858 and became an NHA evangelist. From 1879 to 1886 he was pastor of an independent holiness congregation, the Free Evangelical Church of North Attleboro, Massachusetts. His books, including *Perfect Love*, circulated widely among holiness people. He and McDonald preached in many California churches, and Wood settled in Lincoln Park, by Pasadena. He often preached for Bresee on Sunday evenings. McDonald, Wood, and Bresee were making Pasadena a center of holiness teaching in California Methodism. Bresee encountered minor opposition over the issue, but Pasadena remained a center of the local Holiness Movement after Bresee left. Wood and another Methodist evangelist, Joseph Smith, spoke there well into the 1890s.

Bresee's opposition in Pasadena was not directed so much at his holiness preaching but at him personally, for opposing the liquor traffic. Pasadena's first saloon opened in 1884, and A. W. Bunker, the pastor at the time, joined a rally condemning liquor sales. They visited saloon owner Jerry Beebe, hoping to persuade him to close his shop. Beebe was licensed and had violated no laws, but he offered to sell the saloon for seven thousand dollars! This impasse led to Pasadena's incorporation, which made it possible to pass a local ordinance against liquor sales. New arrivals and new "first class" hotels ran counter to prohibition sentiment, but Dr. Hiram Reid and others organized the "Mutual Protective Association." Supported by the Women's Christian Temperance Union, it petitioned Pasadena's trustees to prohibit the sale of alcoholic beverages.

The clergy supported the petition, and Bresee was at the forefront. He opened his church to a temperance rally in January 1887 and joined the 540 people who pledged to boycott businesses that did not support "Ordinance 39." The ordinance passed. Beebe's successor defied it, was arrested, lost his appeal, and finally moved elsewhere. Still, bitterness lingered over the battle. The law proved unenforceable. Bresee was resented for supporting a boycott designed to intimidate the city's trustees. He remained a strong prohibitionist, believing this to be Methodism's historic position. He carried this emphasis into his new denomination, whose twin purposes, he later said, were holiness and temperance.

Leaving Pasadena

By 1890 prosperity was in the offing, though losses were still larger than gains. Bresee's quarterly reports mention losses due to emigration, but they were leveling off. His May report reflected the signs of change within Methodism. Class meetings were giving way to Sunday school classes, the Epworth League for young people, a businessmen's meeting, and other new groups. Bresee reported that some children's teachers were doing "class leader's work." The quarterly conference minutes for August recapitulate Bresee's Pasadena ministry in a report that became his swan song. The "Sabbath School" (Bresee never used the word "Sunday") had lost members, but the Epworth League was progressing and met on Friday nights and "Sabbath-evening." In his opinion, the Epworth League was functioning like a Methodist class meeting oriented toward the young. Bresee could find value in change. Quarterly membership gains outnumbered losses. Church membership stood at 508, with 25 probationary members. Bresee summarized his Pasadena ministry: "During the last two years we have worked under the influence of a vast receding wave, such as most of us never before experienced. . . . It has taken from us our anointed workers . . . But many anointed souls have gone elsewhere to do valiant service for the Lord and amid it all God has given precious baptisms of the Holy Spirit full upon us."

The church had enjoyed "seasons of great spiritual power," Bresee said, and with the return of prosperity, the future was hopeful. "Let the church be true to God. Let her one aim more than ever be the salvation of the people and the filling this valley with the Kingdom of Jesus Christ. Let her feel the power of her mission to spread holiness over these lands." He thanked "the official brethren" for their "uniform kindness and courtesy," observing that his "term of service had been longer with them than the law ever allowed me elsewhere—so I love them all with an especial love."

The church's recent general conference made it possible to extend pastoral terms up to five years; Bresee had served four. His report was worded as a farewell, with the door open to his possible return for another year. Bresee withdrew for a time so that members could consider the next year's pastoral arrangements. A motion seeking Bresee's return for a fifth year passed unanimously. Then something happened that evidently disconcerted him. Presiding elder J. W. Van Cleve convened an adjourned session of the fourth quarterly conference on September 8. It reconsidered the motion seeking Bresee's return, which carried without any dissenting votes. The minutes state no reason for the action. Girvin says that Bresee felt there was opposition to "the preaching and work of holiness" by some influential members with "wealth and standing"—probably no more than a half dozen persons. "He felt that he could not work advantageously where some of the members were antagonistic to the gospel that he preached."

Bresee had decided to leave Pasadena, a decision regretted by Van Cleve, Bishop Daniel Goodsell, and many church members. It was regretted especially by the Epworth League, which issued an affectionate statement of appreciation for Bresee's work with them and sent copies to the press. According to Girvin, Bresee "subsequently came to see that this was a faulty judgment and a great error" on his part.

NINE

"I AM A METHODIST
PREACHER"

༄

Asbury Methodist Episcopal Church, 1890-91

Bishop Daniel Goodsell presided at the 1890 annual conference in Santa Barbara. Asbury Methodist Episcopal Church's official board heard that Bresee was not returning to Pasadena and invited him as their pastor. Bresee was willing, and Bishop Goodsell concurred.

Asbury was one of Los Angeles Methodism's older churches. In 1882, two Methodists east of the Los Angeles River wanted a church in their area. Lots were donated, and E. S. Chase, pastor at Fort Street, cooperated. A church named for Francis Asbury was organized with eighteen members. It had a new paid building within a year. At some point it received a pipe organ in honor of Henry Sigler, given by his family. In 1890, Asbury reported 229 members and a salary of $1,800. The church was not "flourishing" and its board wanted Bresee to "bring it forward." And yet, some of the same board members agreed among themselves that they would not accept Bresee's message of "full salvation."

Bresee arrived and launched a two-week revival assisted by William McDonald and J. A. Wood. The tide turned on the second Sunday afternoon, when there were "many persons at the altar." Shortly afterward, "one of the leading members of the official board cried to God for full salvation. Amid tears and prayers, he looked up, and seeing some of the brethren of the official board standing by, exclaimed, 'Brethren, you can't depend on me any longer.'" Bresee remembered many conversions and said that nearly all the board members "came into the experience of sanctification."

Other revivals followed. Amanda Berry Smith preached in one of them. Smith was a former slave, a lay evangelist, and a missionary. A member of the African Methodist Episcopal Church, she had gained an international reputation for earnest and eloquent preaching. Bresee had heard her preach before but was still captivated: "She preached one Sabbath afternoon, as I never heard her before, and as I have rarely ever heard anybody preach, in strains of holy eloquence and unction, almost equal to Bishop Simpson in the zenith of his power and sacred oratory." Two preachers professed entire sanctification during Bresee's year at Asbury, including F. Pearl Sigler, who Bresee said "preached the experience up to the time of his death in Kansas City."

Bresee now identified more strongly than ever with the Holiness Movement. He spent nine weeks attending NHA camp meetings in the East and Midwest. Asbury Church's revival spirit continued in his absence, and he and the church sought his reappointment for another year. At annual conference, presiding elder Van Cleve reported that the Asbury Church, under Bresee, had built "a neat little chapel for $400" at its Ela Hills mission. Van Cleve reported 525 conversions on the district that year; Asbury, under Bresee's leadership, accounted for one hundred of these.

The presiding bishop at the 1891 annual conference was Willard F. Mallalieu, longtime advocate of entire sanctification and a Holiness Movement ally on the Board of Bishops. Bishop Mallalieu wanted

Bresee to succeed Van Cleve as the Los Angeles District's presiding elder. Bresee resisted. Girvin says that Bresee "put forth every effort that was possible to avoid having this appointment thrust upon him, but he was unsuccessful." Bresee knew the constant travel and paperwork of a presiding elder and all the quarterly conferences that had to be conducted in the district's thirty-eight churches.

There was also this: "On motion of Doctor Bresee," a committee was raised to plan evening revival services in conjunction with the next annual conference. Bresee was appointed to the committee. He would turn district administration into evangelism and hoped to put the whole conference machinery to the task.

The 1891 annual conference also elected delegates to the 1892 General Conference. Bresee was the first clergy delegate elected, receiving 58 of 115 votes cast on the first ballot. The conference also voted on a constitutional amendment to allow women full rights as lay delegates to the lay electoral conferences and to the denomination's General Conference. Southern California approved the measure by 65 to 39. There is little doubt that Bresee favored the change, but mainline Methodism was far from admitting women into its ministry.

Conference minutes record another thing: Senator Charles Maclay died in July. The veteran minister and businessman had established the conference's seminary. The memorial tribute in the conference minutes was written by three men closest to him: Bresee, university president Bovard, and University Church pastor W. S. Matthew. The network surrounding Bresee was weakening.

Presiding Elder Again

A turning point was coming for Bresee and southern California Methodism. A division began, and Bresee's evangelistic leadership brought the holiness issue to a head, pitting bishop against bishop, pastor against pastor, and the laity against one another. After leaving

Asbury, Bresee convened a group of ministers and laity. He said that he had entered district office "at the point of a bayonet." Were he to go from church to church only handling complaints, then he would resign. "On the other hand, if they would arrange to push the work of real spiritual life and salvation, he would throw himself into it, and do his very best." Bishop Mallalieu concurred with his plan to spend three months holding first quarterly conferences to care for the churches' necessary organization, but Bresee proposed spending the second quarter in evangelistic services, "securing such men as he desired to assist him," and going to churches where his team was invited. Bresee intended spending the final three months conducting fourth quarterly conferences, which were decision points for congregations.

He proceeded at once, using McDonald, Wood, and Daniel Cobb as helpers for three months. The first meeting was held at Asbury Church and the second at North Pasadena, where C. A. Bunker arranged the meeting. The son of holiness stalwart A. W. Bunker, C. A. Bunker prayed all night seeking the blessing of a clean heart. Bresee recounts that "in the morning, with one hand upon the open Bible, where he had been reading the promises of God, and the other upon the open Methodist hymn book—this hand resting upon some of the full salvation hymns of Charles Wesley—God marvelously baptized him with the Holy Ghost and fire, transforming his whole being, and making him, at least for a time, a flaming herald of holiness." The words "at least for a time" express Bresee's disappointment that some preachers backed away from earlier professions of entire sanctification.

Other notables were won to the doctrine. Bresee's meeting at the Vincent Church was attended by S. W. Campbell, the new pastor at Los Angeles First Church (as the Fort Street Church was now called). At Campbell's invitation, Bresee added First Church to the series of sixteen revivals, where some "official members" opposed his doctrine, but the meeting was marked by prayer meetings, testimonies, and Bresee's urgent exhortations. In one service, Campbell left the platform to become a seeker at the altar, followed by many of his members. The meeting was extended an extra week.

Bishop Charles Fowler in San Francisco was a critic of the Holiness Movement. He reportedly called entire sanctification an "intellectual idiosyncracy" and went to Los Angeles hoping to persuade Bishop Mallalieu to remove Bresee from his district office. Mallalieu refused. Bresee's work continued. Holiness was the main topic and passion of many when pastors gathered in April 1892, but not all were persuaded, and opposition developed, some of it carefully plotted and planned.

In May Bresee attended the General Conference of the Methodist Episcopal Church in Omaha. He voted for equal lay and clergy representation at annual and general conferences. The women's ordination issue was also on the floor. One can assume that Bresee favored their ordination; the motion failed, however. Bresee was favorably mentioned in the *Daily Christian Advocate*, the newspaper published during General Conference: "Rev. P. F. Bresee, D.D., of the California Conference, is a man of strong personality. His methods of work are purely evangelistic. The district of which he is the presiding elder is under a general revival influence. He was formerly of the Des Moines Conference and has been on the Pacific Coast about seven years. He leads the delegation from his new Conference. He has peculiar ability as a dedicator." His testimony was also featured. He noted that a few years after his conversion, "I entered into this blessing of entire sanctification." Other testimonies to entire sanctification appeared in the series, including one by his colleague, E. W. Caswell.

Could Bresee have been elected a bishop? He might have been a favorite for many within the Holiness Movement, but there were no vacancies in 1892. The Committee on Episcopacy, on which Bresee sat, rejected a request to increase the number of bishops. The committee also considered a request that the two "missionary bishops," William Taylor and J. M. Thoburn, be classified as "general superintendents" like the other bishops. The committee denied the request, arguing that Taylor and Thoburn had regional, not general, oversight of the church. The committee voted to continue "an itinerant general superintendency." These discussions indicate how Bresee would view the term "general superintendent" as a title in the Church of the Nazarene. In his Nazarene years, he would be an itinerating superintendent of the whole church.

Bresee and Bishop Vincent

After returning from General Conference, Bresee conducted fourth quarterly conferences. The summer holiness work was carried on at Long Beach, but opposition was growing among some "leading ministers of the district" who feared that conference leadership was tilting toward Bresee and his National Holiness Association allies. They took measures to undercut his influence.

The 1892 annual conference was held in San Diego. Bishop John Vincent presided. Vincent, six years Bresee's senior, had similar origins. He descended from Huguenots who settled in New York. His early education was sporadic. He worked in a store and began preaching at eighteen. But his life eventually turned toward education, language study, and travel in Europe and the Near East. Ordained by the Rock River Conference, Vincent was a friend of Ulysses S. Grant. In 1866 he began leading the burgeoning Sunday school movement, training teachers and preparing Sunday school literature. He founded the Chautauqua Assembly, which used camp meeting grounds for "edification or education or both." Vincent personified Methodism's new sophistication and respectability. The leader of Chautauqua confronted the advocate of camp meetings in 1892.

The bishop won, of course. He canceled the evening revival services scheduled the previous year. Bresee arrived early in San Diego
to start the meetings but was the only committee member to do so.
The others had evidently dropped away, perhaps frightened by Vincent. "I held the meeting for several days and nights," he told Girvin,
"and there was a very precious outpouring of the spirit of God upon
the people." But the services stopped once the conference opened.
Vincent silenced Bresee further by ordering that presiding elders
report only in writing, not orally as usual. The written reports are
revealing, but their impact on the assembly was nullified.

Bresee reported:

Gracious revivals have obtained, in most of the churches. The
sanctification of believers, the reclamation of back-sliders and
the conversion of sinners has been the chief work of most of the
pastors. . . . The camp meeting of twelve days was a marvelous
season of grace, reaching in its holy saving influences many of the
charges. . . . The preaching of the Word, love-feasts, class meetings, prayer meetings, all-day meetings, pentecostal meetings
and camp meetings are as in the days gone by in our Church,
seasons of refreshing from the presence of the Lord.

Bresee commended pastors and their families for doing "noble work
on small salaries." He praised the Epworth League and the successes
of "the College of Liberal Arts at West Los Angeles and the College
of Theology at San Fernando."

M. M. Bovard's passing was noted. The first president of the University of Southern California had died in December 1891 at forty-four. Bresee had lost another friend and ally. The university faced
Bovard's death and the prospect of collapsing under an operating
debt of eighteen thousand dollars. They turned to Dr. J. P. Widney,
who had kept the College of Medicine solvent out of his own pocket.
Widney became president upon Bovard's death and immediately

reorganized the structure, creating a separate board for the College of Liberal Arts. Bresee had been vice president of the University Board of Directors since 1884. Now he became chairman of the new separate board. Historian Timothy Smith argues that Widney's purpose was to reestablish the connection between the college and "the spiritual leaders of California Methodism." Under leadership from Widney and Bresee, the College of Liberal Arts found support within the conference. It survived and grew.

Simpson Tabernacle, 1892-93

Bresee told Girvin that Bishop Vincent made remarks in a cabinet session that revealed a personal dislike of the holiness people, and he maintained that Vincent was determined to remove him from the cabinet, which was composed of the presiding elders in the conference. As was customary, the bishop turned to a presiding elder for counsel about appointments. As Bresee related it, Vincent asked: "'Dr. Bresee, who is to go to Simpson church?' I replied: 'I do not know. It is possible they may be compelled to have a transfer.' He then said, 'Why don't you go there yourself?'" But was Vincent demoting Bresee? Hear Bresee's reply: "I answered that I had told the committee which had approached me in reference to the matter, that, if it were thought best by the Presiding Bishop for me to go there, I would serve them to the best of my ability." Bresee had not sought the office of presiding elder and had already consented to become Simpson Church's pastor. The bishop appointed him there. Again Bresee had been sought by a church and expected the bishop to concur.

Simpson Tabernacle's congregation included Judge Robert Widney; Bresee's son, Phineas W.; and Emma Stine, a teacher and the Epworth League's second vice president. Others included Judge William S. Knott, a prominent and affluent attorney, and his wife, Lucy, who came from an old Kentucky family. They were ardent holiness people. Judge Widney and Judge Knott were "official members"— both were trustees and Knott was also a steward. Judge Widney's wife was president of the women's society. Bresee had friends there. His gifts offered hope that the congregation could be built up and Simpson Tabernacle saved from impending financial ruin.

The Bresees moved into the parsonage on South Grand Avenue. Bresee's parents still lived with them, but the only remaining children in the household were Paul, Melvin, and Susan. Bresee entered Simpson's work with energy and vision. He based his first sermon there on Isa. 6:8—"I heard the voice of the Lord, saying, Whom shall I send, and who will go for us? Then said I, Here am I; send me." He spoke:

Why I am here needs no explanation. I am a Methodist preacher, eligible to every appointment in any Conference and liable to any. . . . I never felt called to District work . . . When the invitation [to Simpson] came to me, I at once said if it shall seem providential and the bishop shall see best, I will come. . . .

With this magnificent audience room situated here in the midst of this city, easily accessible, I believed it possible to gather the multitudes here to hear the gospel . . . That here my Lord would walk amid the multitudes to save. . . . I came as sent of God It seems to me that nothing but the over-ruling providence of God has brought me to stand here. I have been hitherto hindered when over and again you have so kindly invited me. And now at this time I have been brought hither, it seems to me entirely providential. . . .

My message is to poverty and distress. . . . My message is to the bereaved, the suffering, and the dying, binding up the broken hearted. . . . My message is to men enslaved, full of worldliness, to hold before their eyes the divine living Christ. . . . Each member of this Church is to be a lodestar.

These words spoke to Bresee's intentions, but how many of the twenty-five hundred seats were filled? Had the tabernacle accomplished its original purpose? And what might that be? A great hall, in the midst of the city, that was a light to all, from children to the elderly, and especially the poor, the suffering, the lonely, the broken-hearted, and those enslaved and "full of worldliness." Such was the soaring vision, but it collided with the reality. Within months Bresee recommended that the church be closed.

The congregation was small and crushed by debt. The national economy was a disaster that year and the following year. Strikes broke out across America, followed by the worst depression since 1837. Trusts and corporations collapsed, leaving thousands jobless. Churches were affected and debts went unpaid. Simpson Tabernacle sank from the plight of the rich, not the poverty of the poor. This had been Bresee's project. An evangelist and chaplain to the Gilded Age, he had worked with wealthy backers in Iowa and California. Now the laity was in financial trouble and Bresee discovered, perhaps for the first time, the enormity of Simpson's financial problems. Perhaps he had taken at face value the report of the presiding elder who had said of Simpson Church in 1891: "Only about $4,500 yet remain to be raised, to relieve this magnificent church of its entire indebtedness."

As rumors spread through the city, Bresee faced them squarely, describing the problem to the *Los Angeles Times* in a report published on January 4, 1893. He had found a small congregation whose members "have manfully borne many heavy burdens." Now they were burdened beyond their strength. They had accumulated new operating debts. Pledges to the building fund seemed "uncollectible." Interest and taxes were accumulating. The debt amounted to thirty-three thousand dollars, which the church could not carry. The options were to "pay the debt" and save the magnificent building for Methodism, or pay the debt *with* the property. But only wealthy men could save it for the church, because the rank and file were financially exhausted. Steps had already been taken to sell the building, which had cost roughly $87,000. Only $47,000 had been paid, and Judge Widney had paid $27,380 of that. Once more, Bresee was appealing to "wealthy men" while defending ordinary and "heroic men and women." Girvin blames members for refusing "to accept the deep things of God" and "enter into the glory and power of Pentecost." It is simplistic. Bresee faced complex factors. At the time, he praised, not blamed, the members.

Financial relief did not materialize. Halfway through the year, Bresee notified the church that he would not return as pastor. Eventually the tabernacle was sold to the Unitarians, who could not handle it, then to others. It became commercial property and was razed after World War II.

TEN
A HEART FOR THE POOR

∽

Boyle Heights Methodist Episcopal Church, 1893-94

Bishop Andrews sent Bresee to Boyle Heights Methodist Episcopal Church on Los Angeles's east side. It had no debt but was behind on operating expenses. Bresee built up the church membership, paid the debt, and left a balance for the following year. Judge William and Lucy Knott followed Bresee there from Simpson Tabernacle.

Bresee's attention was shifting to larger arenas. Boyle Heights became a gathering place for his wider following within southern California's Holiness Movement. His Christmas love feast served this purpose, and he added the observance of Pentecost Sunday, calling it the "anniversary of Pentecost," which was celebrated at Boyle Heights on Sunday and Monday, May 13 and 14, 1894. Evangelists assisted in the preaching.

George Newton reported a "general rally of the saints from the various sections of the city and vicinity," which captures Bresee's design. Newton continued:

> The Lord was present in power in the "Love Feast" sabbath morning and in the preaching of the Word by Bro. Bresee. Sab-

▲ Phineas's childhood home in Franklin, New York. (chapter 1)

Carl and Marjorie Bangs Collection

▲ Bresee's Parents: Phineas Philips Bresee and Susan Brown Bresee. (chapter 2)

Horace and Esther Bresee Collection

▲ The Horace Hebbard residence in 1860, at the time of Phineas and Maria's marriage. (chapter 2)

Horace and Esther Bresee Collection

▲ Bishop Matthew Simpson, one of Bresee's heroes, ordained him a deacon in 1859. Bishop Levi Scott ordained him an elder in 1861. Bresee helped plan two institutions named for Bishop Simpson: Simpson Centenary College in Iowa and Simpson Tabernacle in Los Angeles. (chapter 3)

Simpson, "Cyclopaedia of Methodism," 1878

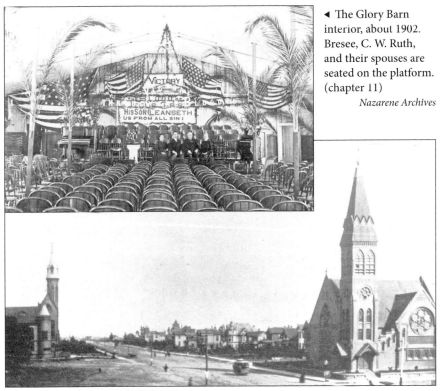

◀ The Glory Barn interior, about 1902. Bresee, C. W. Ruth, and their spouses are seated on the platform. (chapter 11)

Nazarene Archives

▲ Colorado Street in Pasadena, looking east, with the Methodist Episcopal Church on the right. Pasadena's Rose Parade already traveled past this corner during Bresee's pastorate. (chapter 8)

Pasadena First United Methodist Church Archives

▲ William McDonald and J. A. Wood, leaders of the National Holiness Association, helped Bresee promote holiness conventions and revivals on the Los Angeles District while he was presiding elder. (chapter 9)

▲ The Bresee family in 1893. *Upper row:* Bresee's sons: Melvin, Ernest, Paul, and Phineas W. *Middle row:* son-in-law Dr. John Parker, Maria, Phineas P. (holding unidentified child), Susan, Phineas F., and Fred Cowley. *Seated on the floor:* Sue, an unidentified daughter-in-law, and Bertha Bresee Parker. (chapter 10)

Lucy Knott and Judge W. S. Knott were Bresee's parishioners at Fort Street, Simpson Tabernacle, and Boyle Heights, and were charter members of the Church of the Nazarene. Later she became the pastor of the Nazarene congregation on Mateo Street, and in 1903 she became the second woman ordained by Bresee. (chapter 11) ▶

◀ Bresee probably still wore a beard when the Church of the Nazarene was organized in 1895. This is one of the earliest pictures taken after he shaved it. (chapter 13)

◄ Camp meetings were generally conducted in tented cities erected in groves. This scene around 1911, was probably in Pasadena. *Seated:* E. P. Ellyson and P. F. Bresee. *Standing (l. to r.):* Emily Ellyson and three Bresees: Ernest, Ada, and Sue. In April 1908, Phineas Bresee appointed Emily Ellyson as pastor of the Nazarene congregation in Peniel, Texas. He ordained her later that year in the uniting General Assembly at Pilot Point. E. P. Ellyson followed Bresee as president of Nazarene University. (chapter 14)

Nazarene Archives, the Camp Meeting Collection

▲ Bresee and Nazarene University faculty, 1912. Bresee is flanked by president E. P. Ellyson and theology department head H. Orton Wiley, who succeeded Ellyson in 1913. In 1915, a dying Bresee asked Wiley to "stand by the college." Wiley was forced out in 1916, but returned for two other terms as president (1926-29 and 1933-47), guiding Pasadena College during its "glory years." (chapter 14)

Nazarene Archives, Nazarene University Collection

▲ An iconic scene: The Hallelujah March following the successful merger of the North and South, Second General Assembly, October 1908. (chapter 15)

Nazarene Archives

◀ Hiram F. Reynolds had a background in the New England Holiness movement. He became Bresee's fellow general superintendent in 1907 at the First General Assembly in Chicago and continued in office until 1932. He also served as the executive secretary for world missions during much of that time and in 1914 became the first general superintendent to travel around the world. (chapter 15)

The first meeting of the Board of General ▶ Superintendents of the Pentecostal Church of the Nazarene, October 1908, Peniel, Texas. *From left:* E. P. Ellyson, P. F. Bresee, and H. F. Reynolds. (chapter 15)

Nazarene Archives

▲ Phineas and Maria Bresee.
(chapter 15)

Nazarene Archives

▲ Bresee wrote sermons and letters
at his desk in Paul and Ada's home.
Occasionally he chided Horace for
making too much noise. (chapter 16)

Girvin,
"Phineas F. Bresee: A Prince in Israel," 1916

▲ Bresee's funeral at Los Angeles First Church. (chapter 16)

Sue Bresee, whose diaries shed light on family life. (chapter 16) ▶

▲ The Bresees and the Gliddens with Paul, Horace, and Ada. (chapter 16)

◀ "The greatest blessing I have ever had is my wife." (chapter 16)

Nazarene Archives

bath night after a sermon on being "Filled with the Spirit" by the writer to a large and attentive congregation, a large number were at the altar . . . Monday morning at 9:30 people came. . . About 11 a.m., a cloud-burst of glory fell upon all and surely Pentecost was repeated as in the "upper room." Shouts and dancing of saints, weeping and a most remarkable outpouring of the Spirit never to be forgotten by those present was experienced.

Preachers attended the Pentecost meetings, including E. W. Caswell, Santa Barbara District presiding elder. "Holiness evangelism," Newton observed, "is strengthening in these parts."

Then he wrote a sentence almost in passing: "The gospel mission, which Bro. Bresee is to lead after the next session of his conference, planned by Bro. and Sister Ferguson, has just broken ground and will be in readiness by September." Newton referred to the Peniel Mission. Theodore and Manie Ferguson had approached Bresee in early 1894. They were planning a large mission building and program. They had financing. It was to be "undenominational," so Bresee gave little consideration to it at first. They persisted, and Bresee saw the possibility of "a place in the heart of the city, which could be made a center of holy fire, and where the gospel could be preached to the poor." "Agreements were entered into," he told Girvin, "arrangements made, property purchased, in the heart of the city, a block erected." These agreements were with the Fergusons, not with the Southern California Conference.

Newton's connection to Bresee is significant. Newton had left the California Conference in 1876. He operated a mission in San Francisco and edited the *Pacific Herald of Holiness* for the Pacific Coast Holiness Association. The "association"—a middle way between the old denominations and the new ones—brought with it independent missions. Newton argued that associations and missions gave the Holiness Movement institutional form without creating conflict with the churches. Bresee was about to adopt the same strategy. He was on his way to a ministry outside the Methodist system.

The Vortex

Bresee moved into a vortex of four converging currents. He entered it blindly. He was buffeted severely and cast upon uncharted shore. The Peniel Mission was the vortex. The currents were the Fergusons, their English benefactor G. B. Studd, the versatile J. P. Widney, and the Holiness Movement's lay constituents.

Hardin Wallace's holiness revival at Fort Street Church set the first current in motion. The Fergusons professed entire sanctification in these revivals. Theodore Ferguson was converted at Oberlin College. He became a traveling evangelist and then a worker at Newton's San Francisco Mission. He and Manie moved to southern California. They saw the needs of homeless people and started the Los Angeles Mission, renamed "Peniel Mission" in 1891.

Studd provided them a new building named "Peniel Hall." He was one of three sons of Edward Studd, who made a fortune in India and retired to England to be a country gentleman. After their father's conversion, Kynaston (J. B. K.), George (G. B.), and Charles (C. T.) were taken to hear D. L. Moody. They, too, joined the born-again ranks. Edward died, leaving his boys quite wealthy. They were avid cricketers who gained fame playing together at Eton on a team that won a notable match. Their fame increased at Cambridge, where each took a turn as captain of the Cambridge cricket team. Kynaston became Lord Mayor of London. C. T. Studd was a famous missionary in China and Africa. G. B. Studd's travels took him to Los Angeles. Peniel Hall resembled British buildings—a three-story structure with storerooms fronting the street, a row of bedrooms, some apartments, and an auditorium seating eleven hundred people. He was a wealthy Christian who devoted his resources to the poor. He set in motion events that influenced Bresee.

The Widney current stemmed from the ubiquitous and influential Los Angeles family. Bresee and J. P. Widney had worked to save the College of Liberal Arts. Still president of the University of Southern California, Widney agreed to preach in the Peniel Mission and head a medical training program for missionaries.

The Peniel Mission was a gathering place for the holiness people. The laity were increasingly united more by camp meetings than annual conferences, by holiness evangelists more than pastors. They rallied to Bresee's Christmas love feasts, holiness meetings, anniversaries of Pentecost, and "indoor camp meetings." They were not just the poor but the wider holiness people of Los Angeles.

Why did Bresee tie his fortunes to an independent mission? His ministry was marked by a propensity to rely on wealthy people who could provide for the church's material needs: the Red Oak businessmen, investors Joseph Knotts and Jay Cooke, the Council Bluffs business community, banker Henry Sigler, and A. M. Hough—his former pastor who was also a successful real estate investor. Above all, one thinks of Judge Widney. Bresee was beckoned to an enterprise with two wealthy backers: distinguished cricketer G. B. Studd and wealthy polymath J. P. Widney. There was also Bresee's pattern of planning large urban "auditoriums" or "tabernacles." His church at Red Oak was a beginning. The hapless Central Church in Council Bluffs was another. Simpson Tabernacle yet another, though its purpose became confused by debt. The Pasadena tabernacle functioned as Bresee had intended. Peniel Mission promised to be an urban auditorium for reaching the poor, and people throughout southern California could gather in a "center of holy fire" that he had envisaged for earlier tabernacles.

A plan took shape. The mission's superintendents would be the Fergusons, Bresee, and Studd. Bresee would edit the *Peniel Herald* and be the pastor, preaching on Sunday mornings. Widney, a minister on trial in the Methodist conference, would preach on Sunday evenings. Bresee decided to seek an appointment to the Peniel Mission.

The request was unprecedented for Bresee, his conference, and his bishop. He asked presiding elder G. W. White to be appointed to the mission. If not, then Bresee wanted supernumerary status. He was advised that a regular appointment was "impracticable" (Bresee's term). The 1894 annual conference was held at First Methodist Episcopal Church in Los Angeles, with Bishop J. N. FitzGerald presiding. Bresee's request surfaced on the third afternoon in a closed meeting of clergy. The final agenda item was White's motion to grant Bresee supernumerary status. The minutes state: "After discussion, at length, on motion of T. C. Miller, a pastor on the Santa Barbara District, the motion was laid on the table." Bresee's part in the discussion, he told Girvin, was "to reply to some questions asked me by the Presiding Bishop, as to the methods which I purposed to pursue." Bishop FitzGerald was hardly hostile to Bresee. FitzGerald's mother had led holiness meetings since the 1860s, and the bishop conducted them until his own death in 1908. The conference, not the bishop, controlled the conference relations of clergy.

Girvin says that Bresee was rejected by the conference. This is not necessarily so. The request for a regular appointment to the Peniel Mission was impossible under Methodist law. It lacked one essential—an organized Methodist society to which a traveling preacher could be appointed. There was no precedent or provision for another type of appointment. Bresee's request for supernumerary status was difficult but not impossible. The *Discipline* defined a supernumerary relation as an exemption from traveling ministry because of ill health, but Bresee could not plead ill health. "The action of the

Conference," he told Girvin, "placed me in a position where I could not remain one of its members and go on with the work for which I had arranged, without transgressing the law of the church. So after a night of prayer and thought, I told my Presiding Elder that he might ask for me a location." Then Bresee voiced his personal memories and feelings: "I was now out of the Conference. I had been a member of an annual conference from . . . 18 years of age. I had thus held my membership for a period of 37 years. . . . My heart was full of almost unbearable sadness." But had the other clergy rejected him? Actually, there is evidence of their personal support. The conference continued him on the Board of Deaconesses and reelected him to the University of Southern California board and the Long Beach Resort Association. On the motion of his presiding elder, Bresee was granted location.

"Location" is a technical term. Ministers who locate step outside the traveling ministry and annual conference membership, but they do not surrender their credentials or leave the church. Bresee was now a "local elder," related not to the conference but to a local church's fourth quarterly conference. He remained on the rolls, but now as a local preacher. He still held his conference board positions.

Dr. J. P. Widney, president of the university, had felt drawn more deeply into conference life and was received "on trial" in 1893 and placed in the first year of candidacy. In 1894 he advanced to the second year of the course of study. The bishop appointed him again to the presidency of the university. He was a licensed preacher taking his first steps toward ordination.

The Peniel Mission

Peniel Hall was dedicated October 21. At 9:30 a.m. on Sunday, J. P. Widney led a praise service. A choir, orchestra, and soloist performed at the 11 a.m. service. Bresee preached to a full house on Gen.

133

32:30—"And Jacob called the name of the place Peniel: for I have seen God face to face, and my life is preserved." T. P. Ferguson spoke about finances. A hymn written by Manie Ferguson was sung. Studd prayed the dedicatory prayer. The hall was full again at two o'clock. Mrs. Ferguson preached, and there were seekers. T. P. Ferguson led a street meeting in the evening, drawing many to the eight o'clock service, where J. A. Wood preached.

Methodist and secular papers reported the opening. Many Methodist leaders took part in various facets of the mission. One department was the Peniel Missionary Training School. Widney was in charge of a nurses' training course and certificate for those willing to serve communities without doctors and hospitals. Medical students were to gain experience by treating the poor. Bible study was aimed at evangelism and counseling seekers. The mission became a busy place, with several Sunday services and weekday meetings. Bresee preached on Sunday mornings. There were Tuesday holiness meetings. Joseph H. Smith, a national holiness leader, conducted a revival, and Bresee led the love feast on Christmas Day.

In December the leaders announced a plan for "workers" who attended and supported the mission. Something akin to membership was offered for those without church membership and for those who stayed in their churches while working in the mission. The mission's purpose was defined as "Christian service and fellowship." Eight doctrinal points were announced: the inspiration of the Bible, the Trinity, the fall, the atonement, justification by faith, "sanctification by Faith in the cleansing blood of Jesus Christ and the Baptism of the Holy Ghost," the resurrection of the dead, and eternal reward and punishment. Bresee's parents and younger children attended the Peniel Mission, and members of his holiness constituency followed him there. The *Peniel Herald* mentions the Leslie Gay family and W. S. Knott. There were undoubtedly others.

Timothy Smith argues that the circumstance that led Bresee and others to form a new denomination was not conflict with Methodism but conflict within the Peniel Mission. The rift may have begun in May 1895, when A. B. Simpson was brought in as a special worker. Simpson favored divine healing, which was certainly a problem for Widney. Later, both Widney and Bresee were scheduled to be away from Los Angeles. Widney had resigned as university president and planned to spend a year of study on the East Coast. In late July, Phineas and Maria left for the Midwest, where Bresee preached in National Holiness Association camp meetings in Indiana and Illinois. J. A. Wood preached at Peniel Mission in his absence. While away, Bresee was in the company of Bishop Cyrus Foss and Bishop Mallalieu and other Methodist "loyalists" in the Holiness Movement. The *Peniel Herald* published his reports in August and September. He reported attending five camp meetings and preaching almost daily during his trip.

While still in the Midwest, Bresee was shocked to learn that the Peniel Mission's other leaders were terminating their connection with him. Bresee was charitably closemouthed: "As to their course, and the treatment accorded me by them . . . I prefer to draw a veil." It is possible, however, to identify the circumstances surrounding the hidden trouble. Charles Edwin Jones points out that Studd and T. P. Ferguson had backgrounds in the Keswick holiness tradition, with its Calvinist streak. By contrast, Bresee was solidly Wesleyan and Methodist in orientation. At the same time, and possibly related to it, the Peniel Mission had an increasingly missionary emphasis. The *Peniel Herald* in July 1895 listed "branch missions" in San Diego, San Pedro, San Francisco, Juneau, Sitka, and the "Gilbert Isles in the Marianas."

The *Peniel Herald* obliquely announced Bresee's departure in October, stating: "The *Peniel Herald* is two weeks late in its appearance this month owing to some recent changes in the staff of workers at Peniel. The work, however, has been going on uninterruptedly under the blessing of God and it will continue as heretofore, except that it will probably be more of a missionary work even than in the past." Then it says: "Drs. Bresee and J. P. Widney have associated themselves together for Christian work in this city and the former is no longer connected with the work at Peniel. The Lord give them of His best." This is followed by a statement ominously invoking 1 Cor. 4:5: "Judge nothing before the time, until the Lord come, who both will bring to light the hidden things of darkness, and will make manifest the counsels of the hearts: and then shall every man have praise of God."

Bresee had left the security of Methodism for something that had proven illusory. The Peniel Mission was no port in the storm but the storm itself, casting Bresee on unfamiliar shore. Nearly fifty-eight, Bresee was mature and experienced, faithful to his Methodist heritage. Would there be further fruition of this intense and richly blessed ministry? At the moment, he had not yet sensed God's voice saying, as he later reported, "I have given Myself to you."

PART FOUR
CHURCH OF
❧THE NAZARENE❧

ELEVEN

OUT UNDER THE STARS

ברכ

Bresee was widely respected and at the height of his power. He could have returned to the Southern California Conference, but the Christmas love feast crowd was ready to receive him. The holiness people of southern California had gathered with him on Christmas Day, beginning in Pasadena. Bresee was being tested, but the laity resolved his dilemma. Bresee did not "found" a church as much as consent to be the pastor of a church that a host of laypeople were bringing into existence. That fact is central.

A Small Beginning

The laypeople rented Red Men's Hall, a small lodge hall at 317 South Main Street in Los Angeles. Bresee and J. P. Widney agreed to work with these brave souls. A flier spoke of "Christian work, especially evangelistic and city mission work, and the spreading of the doctrine and experience of Christian holiness." The *Los Angeles Times* reported a "New Denomination," saying that "Drs. Bresee and Widney will found a new church." A modest congregation would normally pass unnoticed, but Los Angeles readers knew about Bresee and Widney. There was Widney's service in medicine, civic planning, university education, and service to the poor, and Bresee's service as pastor, presiding elder, temperance reformer, General Conference delegate, and member of numerous boards, including that of the College of Liberal Arts of the University of Southern California.

The first public meeting was on Sunday, October 6, 1895. Bresee's sermon was based on Jer. 6:16: "Ask for the old paths." He said that "the reformers have not led men into new paths, but back to old truths." He deplored the tendency of "light thinkers" to ignore "the simplicity of the gospel." He insisted that "conversion and sanctification must be experienced."

The next Sunday, they announced that the new church would be organized on October 20 and named Church of the Nazarene, which Widney had proposed. The name came to him, he said, after a night of prayer. It symbolized "the toiling, lowly mission of Christ" and linked him to the "struggling, sorrowing heart of the world," which "turns, that it may have hope," to Jesus of Nazareth.

Widney's sermon on October 20 indicates the name's meaning to him. His text was Matt. 4:19, Christ's words to Peter, "Follow me." Widney said:

> Notice that Christ does not say: Accept the creed I frame. Observe the church rituals I devise, or join the church which I found. He only said, "Follow me." It was as though He had said, "Come, live My life with Me." What does it mean? It means that Christianity is not a creed; not a ritual; but a life. Christ had no church edifice for His service; gave no forms save a simple prayer that a child may repeat; framed no formal creed.

The church name conveyed nothing about Methodist doctrine or about holiness. Rather, it expressed late-nineteenth-century "Jesus of history" theology, which preferred the name Jesus to the more exalted Jesus Christ. The Jesus of history was the human person remembered for words and deeds, followed as Teacher and Example, and less the eternal Second Person of the Trinity who made "a full, perfect, and sufficient sacrifice, oblation, and satisfaction for the sins of the whole world." Widney's religious pilgrimage bears out the name's connotation of low Christology and low ecclesiology for him.

Then why did Bresee accept the name? Perhaps he was unaware of the theological fashion surrounding it. Certainly Bresee was fashioning *a church with a theology*, and religious experience was central in both, but it was wrought in the believer by the Second Person of the Trinity, who gives the Holy Spirit. "Church of the Nazarene" expressed Bresee's desire for a church that welcomed rich and poor alike, where all could accept the message of Christ without the encrustations of overgrown ecclesiasticism and formality and without embarrassment over poverty or wealth. He accepted the name without evident reservations.

"Organized Holiness"

Bresee and his friends began enrolling members. The invitation to form the new church was given on October 20. Girvin writes:

At the morning service eighty-six men and women stood together and plighted to God and each other their fidelity in the organization and carrying on of the Church of the Nazarene, with the declared purpose of preaching holiness, and carrying the gospel to the poor. The members were added to, so that during the day one hundred were enrolled, and the list of charter members being kept open for a few days, the organization was finally consummated with 135 charter members

Timothy Smith puts the number at 82, citing no source, but no list of 82, 86, or 135 members has been found. The initial group was never identified in detail.

Some knew Bresee from Fort Street Church, including Alice Baldwin, Judge W. S. and Lucy Knott, and Clarence McKee. The Knotts had also been with Bresee at Simpson Tabernacle and Boyle Heights.

Other early members from Fort Street were Paul Bresee, Leslie Gay, Fred Howland, and Valentine Jacques. The "old guard," though, was outnumbered by younger people, like Emma Stine from Simpson Tabernacle. The non-Methodists included Mrs. Willard, an Episcopalian, and her friend Colonel Duncan. The new church was rich in leadership. Bresee and Widney brought institutional leadership. Knott brought legal talent. Others were businessmen and educators.

The First Structure

The members met on October 30 "to complete the organization of the Church of the Nazarene, elect officers, and take the necessary steps for incorporating under the laws of the State of California." Widney presided. Knott was elected secretary. The meeting adopted articles of faith and bylaws, elected officers, and prepared to incorporate. They said: "We associate ourselves as a church of God under the name of the Church of the Nazarene." Further: "We seek the simplicity of the pentecostal power of the primitive New Testament church. The field of labor to which we feel especially called is in the neglected quarters of the cities and wherever else may be found waste places and souls seeking pardon and cleansing from sin." The agencies of such labors were to be "city missions, evangelistic services, house-to-house visitation, caring for the poor, and comforting the dying."

Each congregation was to have one or more pastors, seven trustees, five to thirteen stewards, and a Sunday school superintendent. Together, these constituted "the official board." The structure was similar to Methodist churches.

So was the official ministry. The Methodist Episcopal Church had two orders of ordained ministry: deacon and elder. The Nazarenes specified only one: the elder. An ordination candidate could be licensed to preach and authorized to conduct worship for one year at a time, subject to general superintendent approval. The meeting agreed to recognize the credentials of ministers uniting from other denominations. Unlike Methodists, though, the Nazarenes affirmed "the equal right of both men and women to all offices of the church, including the ministry." Methodists did not grant women full laity rights until much later, nor did they ordain women as elders until 1956.

Methodist bishops were superintending elders elected for life. Nazarene bylaws also called for general superintendents elected for life. "General superintendent" was a Methodist term for "bishop." Widney and Bresee were named "conjoint pastors of the first congregation" and were to "superintend and direct the general work of the church." Widney, though, was not yet an elder.

Other bylaws made the pastor the president of the official board, insisted that members charged with "immoral conduct or conduct unbecoming a Christian" receive a fair trial, and stipulated that members be received on their promise to observe "the rules and regulations of the church" and their consent to the Articles of Faith.

Articles of Faith

Seven brief Articles of Faith were approved. They resembled the Peniel Mission's eight "points of Christian doctrine." Perhaps Bresee wrote both. They said:

We believe:

1st. In one God, the Father, Son and Holy Ghost.

2nd. In the inspiration of the Holy Scriptures as found in the Old and New Testaments, and that they contain all truth necessary to faith and practice.

3rd. That man is born with a fallen nature, and is thus by nature inclined to evil and that continually.

4th. In the sure loss of the finally impenitent.

5th. That the atonement through Christ is universal, and whosoever hears the word of the Lord and repents and believes on the

Lord Jesus Christ is saved from the condemnation and dominion of sin. That a soul is entirely sanctified subsequent to justification through faith in the Lord Jesus Christ.

6th. That the Spirit of God bears witness in the human heart to justification by faith and to the further work of entire sanctification of believers.

7th. In the resurrection of the dead and the life everlasting.

The articles descended from the Church of England's Thirty-nine Articles of Religion, which John Wesley distilled into Twenty-five Articles for American Methodists. The Anglican and Methodist articles affirm the Trinity first and say that "the Holy Scriptures contain all things necessary to salvation." They speak of "Original or Birth-sin," so that "every man" is "of his own nature inclined to evil." Wesley added the words "and that continually." The "sure loss of the finally impenitent" was assumed in classical orthodoxy and confessed in the Apostles' Creed: "From thence he shall come to judge the quick and the dead." Nazarenes affirmed Wesley's evangelical Arminianism, but Article 5 went further, stating that the atonement holds out hope of entire sanctification for all believers, and that justification and sanctification are received by faith. The witness of the Spirit, found in neither Anglican nor Methodist articles, was a central teaching of Wesley and early Methodism and had official status in Methodism by virtue of being taught in Wesley's *Standard Sermons*. The article on the resurrection and the life everlasting was nearly a direct quote from the Apostles' Creed. These articles tied Nazarenes to the Apostles' Creed, the Nicene Creed, the Reformation, and the Wesleyan Revival.

Article 2 placed Scripture in its historic and orthodox role— providing all things necessary for faith and practice. The articles endorsed no theory of Christ's second coming and ignored the fascination with faith healing (though the church later said something about it). The Nazarene Articles said nothing about sacraments, but the bylaws gave elders "special duties" to administer "the Sacraments of baptism and the Lord's Supper and the solemnization of matrimony." There were no rules of conduct, not even a vestige of Wesley's Rules for the United Societies carried in the Methodist *Discipline*.

The first business meeting elected trustees and stewards. The trustees incorporated the church the very next day, October 31, in the county clerk's office. Bresee probably was not present. His father died that day.

A question arose some years later. When was the church's "birthday"? Bresee answered: the third "Sabbath" of October, the anniversary of that day when the first members came to the front of the little hall to pledge their faith to God and each other.

TWELVE
THE LEADERSHIP CRISIS

༄

Bresee's role was now defined by a denomination he had helped to organize. The official board's first meeting was held November 4 in Widney's office. Bresee presided. The treasurer was directed to pay bills only on the board's instruction. Bresee's salary was to be $125. And it was "Resolved that recognizing the ministry of J. P. Widney as being of God we elect him to Elder's orders in the Church of the Nazarene and that the said credentials be signed officially by the secretary on behalf of the board." Further: "Dr. P. F. Bresee was directed to hold the proper service for setting apart Dr. Joseph P. Widney to elder's orders." Bresee ordained Widney on November 12.

The official board's second meeting, held December 4, instituted the office of deaconess in the Church of the Nazarene. Deaconesses were "to care for the sick and poor, pray with the dying, comfort the sorrowing, seeking the wandering and the lost to bring them to Christ." In January, Arabella Widney presented her deaconess license from the Methodist Episcopal Church and was recognized. Emma Stine and Mrs. Croft were also named as deaconesses. Bresee and Widney were authorized to draw up suitable credentials for deaconesses and elders. Bresee presented his Methodist parchments for deacon and elder; the board accepted their validity. There is no evidence that he ever received a Nazarene parchment, but his Methodist Episcopal parchments are preserved in the Nazarene Archives.

The official board took other important actions in following months. In February 1897 it raised a committee to consider forming other congregations. The general superintendents and others were appointed "to prepare some rules fixing and defining the proper connectional relations of the different churches of the Church of the Nazarene with each other and their pastors." Bresee had already organized a church with nineteen members in Berkeley, California, under pastor Ernest A. Girvin. In March the committee presented six carefully crafted articles granting some autonomy to local churches, including their right to choose their pastors "from time to time," but with the approval of the general superintendents, who could suspend pastors for certain infractions.

The committee recommended that decisions involving all the churches be handled by the concurrence of a majority of official boards, or by "a delegated assembly composed of the pastors of the various churches" and two delegates from each congregation appointed by the official boards. This delegated meeting became the Annual Assembly, and later the District Assembly. Nazarene district and General Assemblies closely paralleled Episcopal Methodism's annual and General Conferences.

The Glory Barn

Two issues became intertwined: obtaining an adequate church building in Los Angeles, and defining Widney's role. The church quickly outgrew Red Men's Hall. Further, neighbors objected to the noisy services. By Thanksgiving, the Nazarenes were in a building between Eighth and Ninth Streets, near the confluence of Spring and Main, but larger quarters were needed. In March 1896, the official board appointed Bresee, Widney, and three laymen to find a lot for erecting a "temporary building." Twelve days later, the board accepted the recommendation to lease a lot between Fifth and Sixth Streets. Loans and pledges were arranged to cover a cost of some eight hundred dollars. Members performed much of the labor. Girvin described the building as "a board structure with sides and roof, but in the mild climate of Southern California, it was sufficiently comfortable. It would seat about 400 people." It was, he added, "little more than a great barn." This structure was the scene of memories that early Nazarenes later held most dear. The "Tabernacle," or "Glory Barn," was formative for their self-understanding and central to their mission and purpose.

The Tempest

Troubling signs surfaced at a "Special Meeting of the Official Board" that Widney convened on September 20, 1897. Bresee was present. Widney wanted to discuss the dissatisfaction "in regard to his aim in building a new church." Board members objected to his intention to hold the property in his own name, not the church's. After hearing objections, Widney said that he was astonished, "since he thought his aim had been clearly understood since the first meeting of the official board. He had sold property to finance a church structure." The board insisted that things remain as they were, and "Widney closed with prayer, thanking God for the union and blessed fellowship that exist amongst us."

He presided again on October 4 and presented written proposals. The church's lease was about to expire, so he and his wife offered to buy a lot and build a church, keeping title to the property "until such time as we may decide otherwise to arrange." The church would use it rent-free for public worship. He proposed an alternative: the Widneys would provide a place of worship but lease it to the church for a nominal sum. If some still objected, then he would remain a general superintendent but go form a second Nazarene congregation in Los Angeles, which he would lead. There was even a fourth plan: he would give the church three thousand dollars to buy a place of worship, while leaving First Church to form a new congregation.

Widney was absent when his proposals were read and discussed on October 11. In a unanimous action, the official board said, "It appears . . . [the Widneys] feel themselves under some kind of obligation to furnish a house of worship for our congregation," but this was not so. Instead, "we think that our church home, when built, should be built from voluntary offerings of all the members, each contributing therefore according to his ability." The board voted to renew the present lease. Bresee and Widney may have understood that Widney would eventually pay for a church building. Bresee had depended on wealthy people to pay for large buildings in Red Oak, Council Bluffs, Pasadena, at Simpson Tabernacle, and at the Peniel Mission.

For a time, there were no further signs of alienation between Widney and the church. Seven months later, he purchased property on Mateo Street, which the church had an option, but no obligation, to buy from him. Worship continued at the Glory Barn, and the board focused on mundane affairs (tuning the organ, buying a bass horn, finding cheaper prices for coal oil, changing to electric lights), handled disciplinary issues, and prepared for a new delegated "assembly" to act for the whole church. But a storm was brewing. It descended on October 10, 1898, one year after the first indications of a rift.

The board minutes of October 17 provide the clearest picture of what occurred earlier. Bresee chaired the meeting. Widney and nearly all board members were present, as was E. A. Girvin from Berkeley. Bresee stated that the meeting was to act on charges made by Widney the previous week. Bresee summarized them:

That the teachings and methods of the Church of the Nazarene were productive of the worst possible results, that they produced simply a lip religion, that they deceived seekers and thus caused wrecked moral and spiritual conditions, that through them souls were being wrecked and were going down to hell. That the wrecked faces haunted him. That our hands were stained with the blood of these souls wrecked because of our teaching and methods. That these things made his blood boil. That he was not angry but he was moved to the depth of his being by these things. That they had gone on from bad to worse until they had broken his heart. That he was going to make an effort at the coming Assembly to reorganize or revolutionize the Church and try to save it from shipwreck. That he stood today with a broken heart in the work. That he had lost confidence in professions of religion [sic] testimony. That he went into this work three years ago with hope but today his heart was broken by the conditions.

Widney responded that Bresee's report, though "somewhat colored," was essentially correct. Widney stood by earlier comments and voiced new objections. Among these was "wildfire." But Widney was vague when board members asked what he meant and who was guilty. Invoking his authority as "one of the joint pastors and Superintendents," Widney called for "radical changes." He wanted "an equal share of the Sunday morning services" and insisted "that this thing of Sanctification must be touched on tenderly."

The board members responded, insisting that the church's teachings and methods had not changed, and that Bresee had used them for many years. One person declared that Widney's charges "were not in any particular true." To the contrary,

the Lord had from the first continuously blessed and owned the work of the Church of the Nazarene in a most wonderful manner; and that Dr. Widney had made his unfounded charges against the Church and in effect warned the public against it as a soul-wrecking institution in the face of these facts and in the midst of one of the most remarkable and blessed series of meetings ever held by any church in Los Angeles.

Someone raised the life tenure of pastors and general superintendents. A board member stated that this "had never been satisfactory" and "had kept persons from joining the church." Bresee replied that such tenure was a "personal matter between himself and Widney" that could be corrected if they both resigned their offices. Bresee offered to resign "if it was thought best." Widney offered to resign, too, if the official board asked for resignations. The board did not lose this momentum and adopted the resolution "that Dr. J. P. Widney and Dr. P. F. Bresee are hereby requested to hand in their resignations as pastors of this church and as General Superintendents of the Church of the Nazarene." Widney wrote the following:

> In compliance with the resolution of the Official Board of the Church of the Nazarene, requesting the resignation of the pastors and General Superintendents, I herewith present my resignation from both offices.

> Oct. 17th 98   J. P. Widney

Bresee worded his resignation differently, sensing that the approaching Annual Assembly representing both the Los Angeles and Berkeley churches was the correct jurisdiction to decide matters of general superintendency:

> I hereby present to you my resignation as pastor of the Church of the Nazarene and as far as this church may have anything to do with it, the General Superintendent.

> P. F. Bresee

A committee was appointed to select a temporary pastor and a temporary editor for *The Nazarene*, a church paper Bresee had begun editing. The minutes record one last item at this momentous meeting: Mr. Shaw was authorized "to have the windows over the choir fixed . . . to prevent a draft blowing on the singers."

The church's first and most unstable period of existence was ending. The initial collaboration of the two leaders was an extension of Bresee's pattern of exercising spiritual leadership while depending on wealthy people to provide finances. But Widney had also assumed the role of a spiritual leader, an irony since the members distrusted the influence of the man with big money. Sanctification was at the center of Bresee's spirituality, while Widney wanted it "touched on tenderly." The core members, drawn from Bresee's former parishioners and those who gathered at the Christmas love feasts, were attached to sanctification in a way that lay outside Widney's ken.

Widney was selfless and generous in his intentions, but he saw himself in the mold of Robert Widney at Simpson Tabernacle and George Studd at the Peniel Mission. The "rising middle-class" members, however, were determined to assume their own financial burden as a sacrifice rather than receive it from someone else's surplus. This surprised Widney. It may have surprised even Bresee.

Widney and Bresee may also have differed in their conversion experiences. Bresee told of his conversion in a class meeting in Davenport, New York, and his sanctification in Chariton, Iowa. No such stories come to us from Widney, suggesting that he did not confess his faith in these terms.

In November the board read a letter from Widney: "Dear Brethren, As the title of the Mateo Street property is rested in me, will you kindly designate some person or persons to whom I may legally transfer the same. Your brother in Christ, J. P. Widney." There was no ill will or lack of generosity in Widney's words or actions. His scruples about the church's direction were honest, and he was faithful about keeping his financial agreements.

Widney After 1898

Widney and Bresee now drifted apart. Each was free to develop his own style and interest. Widney started a new mission in Los Angeles in early 1899 and the Methodists admitted him as a minister by the Southern California Conference in September, upon the transfer of his Nazarene elder's orders. Appointed to his own "City Mission," presiding elder G. F. Bovard reported one year later that Widney

> has faithfully carried out plans which he had originated prior to the time of his appointment. He has invested of his own means more than $6,000 in a building admirably arranged . . . and has organized a society of about 40 members, which he designates as the Nazarene Methodist Episcopal Church. He has a Sunday School of about 60 scholars. In addition to the regular work, as pastor of this new society, he conducts Bible readings in various parts of the city . . . The building . . . is his own private property.

Widney was tolerated for his many contributions to local Methodism, but the arrangement could not last. He soon left Methodism altogether. He wrote books that combined politics, history, and culture, laced with mysticism and a core theme of Aryan racial theory. He developed a syncretistic religion followed by relatives and friends in his privately built "Beth-El, a Chapel and Manse of the Church of the All-Father" (or "All Fader"). A generous, kindly, spiritual adventurer, he was blind in his final decade. Beloved by family and friends, he lived into his ninety-seventh year, dying July 4, 1938.

The Los Angeles Medical Association and the Medical School of the University of Southern California honor him as their founder. The numerous articles about him rarely mention his Nazarene years, but historian Sandra Sizer Frankiel revived interest in him as an example of California's "new mysticism," though she wrongly calls him "an influential California minister."

The Widneys and Bresees reunited in 1909. Maria Bresee wrote about it: "Dr. B and I went out to call on Dr. Widney. He had said he wanted us to come—Sister Melville told us several times, said he was so anxious we should come—we had such a nice friendly call. Miss Belle came in just as she used to be. And Mrs. Will Widney was there too, it was all very nice. Belle enquired very kindly after him [Bresee]. He [Widney] took us in and showed us his new church &c." Widney later sent the Bresees a booklet of his poems.

THIRTEEN

PASTOR TO THE PEOPLE

ᴄ♫ᴐ

Bresee now guided the church through the period that West Coast Nazarenes would regard as their "Golden Age," an era to which they returned in their memories as the Nazarene glory days.

Bresee presided when the official board met again a week after the fateful meeting. The special committee to select a temporary pastor recommended "Dr. P. F. Bresee." The board also returned him to his position as editor of *The Nazarene* and requested that he print one of his sermons in each issue. The question of general superintendency did not arise; it was now in the hands of a delegated assembly.

The First Assembly and the First Manual

In June, the board had appointed Bresee, Widney, J. P. Coleman, and W. S. Knott to revise the Articles of Faith and General Rules. The general superintendents subsequently scheduled an assembly to meet in October, which it did on the 14th and 18th. The first session followed Widney's public meeting of the 10th, when he aired his grievances. The second session met the day after Widney and Bresee resigned. In the second session, the assembly accepted both resignations from the office of general superintendent. It then set the term at one year and elected Bresee to the office. He was out of office less than a day.

Girvin wrote that the necessary revisions had not yet been completed, but a *Manual* later appeared, its title page reading: "The Manual of the Church of the Nazarene. Promulgated by the Assembly of 1898 held in Los Angeles, Cal." The preface was signed "In behalf of the Assembly, P. F. Bresee, Gen'l Sup't."

The *Manual* repeated much of what the first congregational meeting had adopted in 1895, but there were new actions providing for more than one church and for delegated assemblies. The Articles of Faith and General Rules were unchanged, but a new statement on "Christian Perfection" appeared. Perhaps it was inserted lest anyone claim, as Widney had done, that this doctrine was not closely defined. The new statement represented the position of Bresee and the early Nazarenes:

> We believe in the doctrine of Christian Perfection, or Entire Sanctification. That it is a second definite work of grace in the heart, whereby we are thoroughly cleansed from all sin. That only those who are justified and walking in the favor of God can receive this grace. That it is not absolute perfection, that belongs to God alone. It does not make a man infalable [sic]. It is perfect love—the pure love of God filling a clean heart. It is capable of increase. It prepares for more rapid growth in grace. It may be lost, and we need to continually watch and pray. It is received by faith. It is accomplished by the baptism with the Holy Ghost and fire, which is the baptism of Jesus Christ, foretold by John the Baptist. It is loving the Lord our God with all the heart, soul, mind and strength, and our neighbor as ourselves.—Matt. 22:37-39. It was this which the Apostles and Disciples received in the upper room at Jerusalem on the day of Pentecost, for which Jesus commanded them to wait. It is the inheritance of the Church, and with it comes preparation and

anointing and power for the work to which God has called us. Our preachers are to definitely preach it, and urge it upon all believers. It is the privilege and duty of all believers to seek and obtain it. It is this to which we are called: "That we might be made partakers of His Holiness." Heb. xii. 10.

The *Manual* contained "Special Advices" that were urgent in tone. The first stated that "total abstinence from all intoxicants is the Christian rule for the individual, and total prohibition of the traffic is the duty of civil government." Voters were advised to cast their ballots wisely in this regard. Engaging in the liquor traffic "can but be considered a misdemeanor." "Only unfermented wine is to be used in the Sacrament of the Lord's Supper." Another advice said that tobacco was "injurious . . . an offense to many . . . unbecoming in a Christian and a thing to be put away." Christians "should not use it" or traffic in it.

Christian giving was "a duty and a privilege." Christians should marry "only in the Lord" and not unite with unbelievers "in this most sacred and intimate relation." Ministers "should not solemnize marriage" where a divorced spouse was living, except for the innocent party in a divorce caused by adultery, or in the case of a divorced couple who remarried.

Baptism could be administered to adults and children alike. The mode could be "sprinkling, pouring, or immersion, according to the choice of the applicant." Where there was uncertainty, new scruples about mode, or a lack of proper instruction, baptism could be administered again "without regard to previous baptism."

In the ritual for receiving new members, candidates were asked if they "heartily believe" the "essential doctrines of the Church," which are "few and brief": those regarding the Trinity, sin, the need of regeneration, "the further work of heart cleansing or entire sanctification," the witness of the Spirit to these "works of grace," and eternal rewards and punishments. The ritual required a testimony that Christ "saves you now," and new members promised their loyalty to the church. No testimony to entire sanctification was required, as it was in the Holiness Church of Southern California.

The chapter on "Church Membership" followed Wesley's "General Rules of our United Societies" carried in Methodist Episcopal *Disciplines* from the beginning. Many *Manual* readings were identical to Wesley's General Rules, some were paraphrases, and some items were added. Wesley spoke simply against "the taking of such diversions as cannot be used in the name of the Lord Jesus," but the Nazarene *Manual* had strictures against "the theater, the ball room, the circus and like places, lotteries and games of chance."

The ritual for infant baptism was taken from the *Discipline*, down to concluding with the Lord's Prayer. The first paragraph in the ritual for adult baptism was innovative, stating that baptism is "the external seal of the New Covenant," while "the internal seal" is "the baptism with the Holy Ghost and fire."

The *Discipline* followed the Book of Common Prayer and ancient practice in asking new members about the Apostles' Creed in a series of questions and answers. The *Manual* conflated this into one question: "Do you believe in God the Father, and in Jesus Christ His only begotten Son our Lord, and do you believe in the Holy Ghost, the Comforter?" Two other questions followed: "Have you saving faith in the Lord Jesus Christ?" and "Have you received the Holy Ghost since you believed—if not, do you now present yourself a living sacrifice to be cleansed from all sin?" If necessary, water baptism then followed, using the ancient Trinitarian formula.

The ritual for the Lord's Supper was brief, but its continuity with Anglican liturgy and Methodist *Discipline* is again evident. The service "shall be introduced," says the *Manual*, by appropriate preaching and Bible lessons. The minister was to read an invitation to the standing congregation. The *Manual* added a reference to "the memorial of the death and passion." The *Discipline* followed the Book of Common Prayer and proceeded to the "General Confession" said by minister and people. The *Manual* said simply: "The minister, with the congregation, may offer prayer of confession and supplication." The prayer of consecration, abridged in the Methodist *Discipline* from the Book of Common Prayer, was spelled out in the 1898 *Manual* with further abridgment.

The continuity was striking at the point in the service where the elements were to be partaken. The presiding minister was to partake first, and then—with other ministers and stewards—administer Communion to the kneeling congregation. The words of distribution were identical to those of the Methodist ritual.

The Methodist service, like the English liturgy, ended with the Lord's Prayer, a prayer of thanksgiving, and the "Glory be to God on high," concluding with the benediction, "The peace of God . . ." The *Manual* says briefly: "Repeat the Lord's Prayer or extempore prayer of thanksgiving."

Pastor and People

The pastor and people of the Los Angeles Church of the Nazarene were bound in a unique relationship. Methodist evangelist Joseph H. Smith visited the church shortly after 1900 and was favorably impressed. A Methodist loyalist, he did not want to encourage others to separate from Episcopal Methodism, so he noted that other Nazarene congregations did not enjoy the same "phenomenal success" as Bresee's church. Bresee, he said, was the essential factor, for he was

a rare man. Besides the power and life of holiness, he also possesses abilities and experiences which few, even of holiness men and ministers possess. . . . His own ministry in the Methodist church, both as pastor and presiding elder, was always likewise phenomenally successful, and in several instances quite extraordinary. His energy, his endurance, his experience, his manly might and wisdom and tact qualify him for the mastery of men, the management of interests, the prevention of fanaticism, the holding of all sweetly and strongly to the essential interests as only a providential general can do.

Smith also praised the "great number of choice and devoted spirits" who were Bresee's colaborers.

The Sabbath

A distinctive feature of the Los Angeles church was the frequency of its public services. Sunday—Bresee called it the "Sabbath"—was taken up with meetings. A church pamphlet from 1895 listed a schedule that began with the Young Men's Prayer Meeting at 9 a.m., Sabbath school at 9:45, preaching by Bresee at 11:00, a general meeting conducted by Widney at 3:00 p.m., a street meeting at 7:00, and a mass meeting at 7:30. The young men's prayer meeting was described as "full of interest." The "Sabbath School" had an "efficient corps of officers and teachers." Morning worship was "a crowded service, and often a season of great blessing." In the earliest years, people brought their lunch and ate in the pews after the morning service.

Widney's Sunday afternoon series, "Walks with the Nazarene," were "readings and studies in the life and teachings of Jesus. The object is to go directly to Christ's own words and life for His doctrines, and for His message to the world." After Widney's departure, this service featured general testimonies, and later the sermons of guest preachers and associate pastors. It alternated between the love feast and the sacramental service (Lord's Supper). The love feast was primarily for testimonies. The Communion service also allowed for testimonies. Both often ended with altar calls and prayer with seekers for "pardon or purity."

Sunday evening's service was "a mass meeting, with singing, praying, a short address and testimony, with altar and other services."

Other Days of Worship

There were regular weekday activities. Tuesday afternoon featured the holiness meeting in the tradition of Phoebe Palmer's Tuesday Meeting that began in the 1830s. The first pamphlet called it "a meeting of great importance. It has been going on for the year past, and was simply transferred to our hall when we began the Church of the Nazarene, which accounts for its large attendance. The doctrine of entire sanctification is clearly taught, and its experience sought and found " The "transfer" was from the Peniel Mission.

Tuesday holiness meeting testimonies were reported in *The Nazarene*. "Sister Bresee" (Maria), for example, reported: "I have learned something of this second work of grace. The Spirit led me by degrees until I saw it was my privilege to enter in; I now rejoice in the liberty of the children of God." Sister Margaret Dangerfield testified that she was sanctified at Fort Street. There were often seekers for the new birth or for entire sanctification. One meeting began with an infant baptism and the reception of a new church member. The Tuesday Meeting was informal and versatile.

On Thursday the street meeting at 7 p.m. was followed by the "mid-week meeting" at 7:30. Actually several street meetings occurred simultaneously, and people were asked "to join one of the bands." After the Tuesday holiness meeting was discontinued, the Thursday meeting shifted to Wednesday.

The entire membership was enlisted for a time as the Buttonhole Brigade for inviting others to church services and to Christian faith. There was Company A, Company B, and so on. Only Company E survived. It was the young women's group. The young men's group was called the Brotherhood of St. Stephen. Both groups were large and active, conducting street meetings and other services. They trained young people in Christian service and leadership.

The congregation held an "anniversary home campmeeting" each October. It celebrated the church's founding and ran from the first Sunday in the month through the third, reminding members of the two weeks in 1895 that preceded the church's formal organization. These evangelistic services were reminiscent of nineteenth-century outdoor camp meetings. Amenities were nearly as crude during the Glory Barn years. When the church began holding annual assemblies, the anniversary camp meeting began prior to assembly and continued during it. The anniversary home camp meeting was canceled in 1902 because the event had grown too large for the Glory Barn.

Civil holidays provided other opportunities for all-day meetings. Memorial Day and Independence Day yielded celebrations both patriotic and evangelistic. New Year's Eve was marked by a watch night service. On Christmas Day, the church held a Christmas love feast until Bresee's death.

Public Gatherings

The church was the site of frequent temperance rallies, often on Sunday evening. Temperance lecturers drew interdenominational audiences. Dr. Stephen Bowers, the Methodist minister who once led the southern California temperance movement and edited its *Christian Voice*, had joined the Church of the Nazarene by October 1900. Bresee often stated that the Church of the Nazarene was a temperance or "prohibition church."

Funerals were another significant public meeting. The membership included elderly veterans of the Holiness Movement, and the public recollections of their "pilgrim's progress" was a means of indoctrination and evangelization, even as their obituaries in the *Nazarene Messenger* perpetuated the testimony of their lives.

Methodists often requested that Bresee conduct their funerals. Dr. Michael Everley Whisler's funeral was at the Church of the Nazarene, Bresee presiding, assisted by R. S. Cantine, Whisler's Fort Street Church pastor. Bresee also participated at Methodist churches in the funerals of former parishioners. Bresee officiated at the funerals of his mother and that of Demoss La Fontaine, wife of Bresee's cousin and mother of C. V. La Fontaine, Bresee's assistant pastor. Bresee conducted some funerals at funeral parlors—often at Bresee Brothers Mortuary, operated by his sons.

The annual Sunday school picnic was perhaps the most inclusive and largely attended event on the congregation's calendar. The church family gathered and rode by chartered train or streetcar to their destination. Sometimes they went to a park, such as Griffith Park, but more commonly it was to the seashore. In 1902 the picnickers were carried by steam launch to Terminal Island, where "special arrangements for bathing" had been made. Between six hundred and seven hundred people attended. The day closed with a service in which one person professed conversion; another professed entire sanctification.

They returned to Terminal Island in 1903. Bresee closed the day with a Bible reading and an invitation. "Two came and were gloriously blest," said the reporter. "The glory of the Lord came over the people like the wave of a great ocean." The first Nazarene songbook, published two years later, was called *Waves of Glory*.

The report on the 1908 picnic bears repeating: "The annual picnic of the First Church Sunday school was enjoyed at Playa Del Rey, on Thursday, July 23. Several cars loaded with the friends conveyed them to the beach, where a pleasant day of boating, bathing, and fishing was enjoyed. A very enthusiastic and spiritual service was led by General Superintendent Reynolds, who gave a brief gospel message, after which a season of testimony was enjoyed and three souls sought the Lord. After this service two persons were baptized by Dr. Bresee, and soon after the friends returned to the city without incident, all having thoroughly enjoyed the day." A complete picnic—friends assembling to board chartered streetcars, the beach, boating, bathing, fishing, singing, sermon, testimonies, seekers, baptisms, and the happy streetcar ride home again, with singing.

Crosscurrents and Countercurrents

Having repudiated the formalism of the old churches, Bresee also had to resist the fanaticism of unbridled emotionalism. He welcomed warm and exuberant expressions of religious victory but was attacked by radical holiness factions like the "Burning Bush" people (the Metropolitan Church Association) for insisting on order amid religious joy.

Some wanted the Church of the Nazarene to be a platform for speculation about "dispensations" and "last days." Asked if he believed in "the second, literal, personal coming of Christ," Bresee answered affirmatively but added: "There are different theories . . . classified as pre- and post-millennial. As I have read the New Testament I have not found that any special stress is laid upon the time of His coming—only its certainty." He said that the "dispensational truth" is that Christ baptizes us with the Holy Spirit. This is present; it does not await the future.

"Divine healing" was another current attracting followers, perhaps in reaction to Christian Science but also in resistance to scientific medicine. Bresee treated it coolly and welcomed the professional services of his son, Dr. Paul Bresee.

Presbyterians were spreading a theory of Scripture's verbal inerrancy at this time. The *Nazarene Messenger* occasionally mentioned attacks by others on the theory of evolution, but Bresee made little of such polemic. He refused to make the Bible, or even the New Testament, the primary authority for Christians:

We do not go to the documents for the evidence of the truth of our religion. The Church of God was in the world before there were any documents. The Christian church was in the world before the New Testament was written. The great evidence that Christ is God, and the Savior of men, is that He saves them. Men know in their own consciousness that they are saved, and their transformed lives proclaim to all that Jesus lives to save.

Amid these crosscurrents, Bresee appealed to the formula of the sixteenth-century Lutheran Petrus Meiderlinus: "In essentials unity, in non-essentials liberty, in all things charity [love]." This formula had been used by Dutch Remonstrants, Moravians, Richard Baxter, Campbellites, Quakers, and Catholics. It solved nothing in itself but indicated Bresee's simple desire to lead a movement that was firm at the center of its doctrine of sanctification while allowing freedom "around the edges." He stated once that Paul was a "radical-conservative," not merely a conservative. For Bresee, the Christian faith was best conserved by a radical cure of inbred sin. Radicalism for its own sake, he thought, was egoistic fanaticism.

Bresee had to reckon with the rise of modern Pentecostalism, a new and growing religious movement with Los Angeles as an early center. "Tongues-speaking" had recurred throughout church history, but a new phase began on the eve of 1901 at Charles Parham's independent Bible school in Topeka, Kansas. A woman testified that she was given the gift of speaking Chinese. Parham's school moved to Texas a few years later. One student there, William J. Seymour, went to Los Angeles and promoted tongues-speaking at an independent mission. In April 1906, the meetings moved to Azusa Street, not far from the Church of the Nazarene. Sensational accounts of the "Azusa Street revival" appeared in newspapers, swelling the crowds and attracting international attention. The "tongues movement" soon spread to other American cities and abroad. Tongues-speakers claimed to re-create the first Pentecost. The Azusa Street people called their "tongues" a "Pentecostal" gift, and the necessary evidence of the "baptism of the Holy Ghost."

Bresee followed Phoebe Palmer's (but not John Wesley's) practice of referring to entire sanctification as the baptism of the Holy Ghost (from Acts 1:5). So did the Holiness Movement generally, which used Pentecost in its church names. In 1907, Bresee's group merged with the Association of Pentecostal Churches of America, creating the Pentecostal Church of the Nazarene. In 1915, Pentecostal Nazarenes absorbed the Pentecostal Mission and the Pentecostal Church of Scotland. Just before the 1908 merger with the Holiness Church of Christ, J. B. Chapman noted that the merging churches had different names with exactly the same meaning: "Pentecostal means Holiness; Nazarene means Christ." But the popular mind increasingly associated "Pentecostal" with tongues-speaking, as the Pentecostal Church of the Nazarene acknowledged in 1919 when dropping the word from its name.

This lay in the future. What was Bresee's response to early Pentecostalism? The *Nazarene Messenger* noticed tongues-speaking in 1901, when evangelists Herbert and Lillie Buffum reported a visit to Charles Parham in Topeka. After holding a meeting in Omaha, Herbert Buffum told of a woman who was sanctified: "The laughing blessing came upon her and she nearly lost her strength." The Buffums eventually left the Nazarenes to work with the tongues movement.

In 1902 Bresee preached a sermon on the ancient church at Corinth: "Those possessed of the more showy gifts, such as miracles and tongues, became too fond of displaying them and turned them into grounds of boasting; especially the gift of tongues, which led to uproar and confusion." Silent at first about the Azusa Street revival, Bresee finally commented in the *Nazarene Messenger*: "Some months ago . . . there began something which was called the 'gift of tongues.' . . . The professed gift of tongues was not the only peculiarity of the meetings, but much physical exercise of various kinds, with laying on of hands. The meetings attracted some attention, especially among that class of people who are always seeking some new thing." The Azusa Street meetings helped convert sinners and sanctify believers, but so did the Nazarenes. Insofar as the Pentecostals produced fanaticism and heretical teaching, however, Bresee did not want to give them "the prominence of public discussion." Pentecostals had sent exaggerated accounts to "editors in the East." Bresee described things more modestly: "Locally it is of small account, being insignificant both in numbers and influence. . . . The speaking in tongues has been a no-thing—a jargon, a senseless jumble, without meaning to those who do the mumbling, or to those who hear. . . . [when] the speaker or some other one has attempted to interpret, it has usually been a poor mess." He said that true believers "do not hanker after strange fire, nor run after every suppositional gift, nor are they blown about by every wind of doctrine."

A fiction grew up, promoted by Pentecostal writer Stanley Frodsham and perpetuated by others. It held that Nazarenes had invited Seymour to Los Angeles and then barred him from their church after hearing his message The fiction captured the Pentecostals' conviction that the holiness churches had ignored the authentic baptism of the Holy Ghost. It served a polemical interest but was completely false. Today's Pentecostal scholars no longer perpetuate it, though some careless writers still do so.

FOURTEEN

SHAPING THE BODY OF CHRIST

⌥

Bresee's Understanding of Worship

The Church of the Nazarene differed from most Los Angeles churches in the frequency of its public gatherings and the intent and nature of its meetings. The difference arose in the underlying understanding of public worship. Nazarene gatherings were expected to be occasions for personal and corporate joy. Members worshipped rejoicing in the sense of sins forgiven, hearts freed from the recurring selfishness of the "carnal nature," and fresh "anointings" by the Spirit that renewed and deepened the way of holiness. They came expectantly, welcoming kindred spirits and hoping that the service would yield spiritual victories.

Nazarenes respected traditional worship forms but were interested more in the spiritual vitality that had produced them. Bresee, a master of ritual, was not ritualistic. He regarded old church formality as stifling to the life that once enlivened the forms. A public invitation was issued to seekers of forgiveness and purity in nearly every worship service. People were expected to seek God wherever Christians gathered.

Bresee's Personal Bearing

Bresee brought a dignified but vibrant bearing to these gatherings. He greeted people as they entered the Sunday morning service and remained by the pulpit and altar after the service. He presided with a powerful calmness. His sermons were carefully prepared, the text sprinkled with lead-in sentences.

Bresee's sermon delivery was marked by intensity. He was known as a dramatic preacher even in Iowa. One dramatic sermon was on Psalm 23. Bresee had two young men stand behind and follow as he paced back and forth across the platform, preaching. This drew rapt attention. Then came verse 6: "Surely goodness and mercy shall follow me all the days of my life."

Bresee never succumbed to intense emotion but did not discourage emotional responses. Services, even sermons, often were punctuated by spontaneous testimonies, shouting, the waving of white handkerchiefs (commonly done at patriotic and political rallies), and songs. High moments were punctuated by marching around the aisles. In later years, Bresee asked the congregation to stand and march when the service had settled down too much.

Baptism

Like Methodists, Bresee baptized infants, children, and adults. He permitted candidates to choose their mode of baptism. He also allowed rebaptism when it was sincerely requested. His theory and practice were personal and pragmatic. He was determined that the Church of the Nazarene not be divided by issues not germane to its central purpose.

Bresee baptized children throughout his ministry. On Easter Sunday 1904, "Dr. Bresee baptized some children and received some members into the church." Two years later, "at the opening of the morning service Dr. Bresee administered the sacrament of baptism to the infant daughter of Rev. and Mrs. Hendricks, and also to Armour James McFarland." He baptized one child at a college convocation and baptized children at district assemblies. Alan Bresee Smith was baptized in such a setting: "The date of my baptism was November 14, 1914 . . . at a district assembly in Bethany, Oklahoma, where Bresee was presiding. . . . Unexpectedly, right in the middle of things, the obstreperous 15-month-old kid began to flail his arms and legs about and to yell bloody murder. Bresee, a frail old man, was unflappable and fully equal to the occasion. He was sitting in a chair. Placing the child firmly between his knees he baptized him." Smith had been named Allen Cleveland Smith, but when Bresee asked, "What is the name of this child?" Smith's mother responded, "Allen Bresee Smith." He bore the revised name thereafter (and changed the spelling of his first name). At the 1915 Southern California District Assembly, A. M. Bowes, San Diego First Church pastor, wrote in his diary: "In the afternoon Dr. Bresee baptized our baby and several others." The baby, Alpin P. Bowes, was not quite four months old.

Bresee baptized one man at a meeting of the official board, probably by sprinkling. Other baptisms occurred at the seashore, where the mode was probably by immersion in the surf. In 1906 the church announced that "a baptismal service at the beach will be arranged soon." Nine people were baptized one Sunday afternoon in 1899 in the Glory Barn. In 1902, assistant pastor C. W. Ruth baptized sixteen people by immersion at First Methodist Episcopal Church, where the new building contained a baptistery.

Bresee's comprehensive attitude toward baptism was tested at one point, and here he made a concession. The 1898 *Manual* ritual for baptism was in the section on Special Advices:

VI. Baptism.

Water baptism is the formal application of water to the person in the name of the Father, the Son and the Holy Ghost, and is a symbol of the purifying work of the Holy Spirit. Adult believers are proper candidates, also young children, one or both of whose parents or guardians becoming sponsors for their faith and covenant.

Mode.

Baptism may be administered by sprinkling, pouring, or immersion, according to the choice of the applicant.

Re-baptism.

Where on account of uncertainty, or lack of proper instruction, or scruples having arisen as to mode, a person has become conscientiously desirous for the ordinance, it may be administered to them without regard to previous baptism.

The section on "Mode" remained unchanged in later *Manuals*, but other sections were altered. The 1903 *Manual* dropped rebaptism, while the 1905 *Manual* restored it in shortened form. The 1905 *Manual* expanded the basic definition of baptism: "Baptism, by the ordination of Christ, is to be administered to repentant believers as declarative of their faith in Him as their Savior, for the remission of sins unto salvation, and the full purpose of obedience in holiness and righteousness. Baptism being the seal of the New Testament, young children may be baptized upon request of parents or guardians, who shall give assurances for them of necessary and Christian teaching."

This stood until the 1907 merger with the Association of Pentecostal Churches of America. Horace Trumbauer attended the uniting General Assembly in Chicago. He led the Pennsylvania Conference of the Holiness Christian Church and wanted to negotiate his group's union with those uniting in Chicago. Trumbauer was invited to participate in committee work:

I was admitted to the secret session of the commission of 14 or 15 men whose work it was to formulate discipline. I objected to wording in Art. on Baptism, which they struck out. They also inserted a proviso that ministers need not baptize by a mode contrary to their convictions.

I declared my opposition to Infant Baptism on the ground that it is not found in Scripture. "You say you could not baptize infants?" asked Dr. Bresee. "No, sir." "Well, would you object to someone else doing it?" Again I said, "no." What else could I say?

What words were struck out? Trumbauer's diary records the answer: "They struck out for me the words 'for the remission of sins unto salvation.['] It had already been adopted by the body." Trumbauer joined a church that baptized infants, while the church struck the words linking baptism to the remission of sins and agreed to permit ministers to practice only the modes of baptism that their consciences allowed. Trumbauer's conference became the Philadelphia District of the Pentecostal Church of the Nazarene. Bresee, the mediator, compromised so long as unity on essentials was not sacrificed.

The Church of the Nazarene made a later concession to those who emphasized believer's baptism by instituting a ritual for "infant dedication" in 1936, long after Bresee's death.

The Lord's Supper

Bresee followed Methodism's historic form in celebrating the Lord's Supper, but he celebrated the sacrament more frequently and with greater freedom. In 1900, while still in the Glory Barn, the Lord's Supper was evidently combined with the love feast, the celebration of both occurring one Sunday afternoon a month. After the congregation moved in 1903 to a new building, the Lord's Supper was observed twice a month. Annual assemblies, instituted in 1898, began with the Lord's Supper like the Methodist annual conference. Bresee's Communion ware consisted of a silver pitcher and chalice for the juice and a plate for the bread. He occasionally administered Communion in private services to the sick.

The freedom permitted in "the sacramental service" allowed for responses from the congregation. "The Sacramental Service Sabbath afternoon at First church was a season of remarkable blessing, several saying it was the best sacramental service they ever attended," according to a report in 1899. A few months later, the *Nazarene Messenger* reported seekers at the altar after "the Sacrament of the Lord's Supper."

In 1901, "hundreds of people gathered in solemn awe at the table of the Lord; and the presence of the Master in the midst was very blessedly manifest." Was the language of "presence" deliberate or simply a casual way of speaking of a memorial? There is a clue in this report from the Mateo Street Church: "A Sacramental service was held at Mateo Street on Sunday night. It was not a memorial alone, for in the midst was the manifest presence of the risen Lord." Bresee was not speaking of a "real presence" localized in the bread and wine but of a palpable real presence of Christ in the lives of believers present at the service. And yet he knew the issue of the real presence and took sides against a merely memorialist view of the supper.

The Altar

The altar had an important place in Nazarene experience. It was the rail where seekers knelt to pray for pardon and purity. Catholics, Anglicans, and early Methodists regarded the altar as the table on which Eucharistic bread and wine were placed. The railing was the "altar rail." For Bresee, the rail itself was the altar. He wrote: "What we sometimes call an altar is simply a 'mourner's bench' or a 'penitent form,' a place where those who are seekers after God can have special opportunity to pray, and be prayed with and for." In the Lord's Supper, Nazarenes gathered at the very place where many had become believers, and the "altar" was hallowed by their faith, not vice versa. The altar call was not to be treated carelessly. Bresee warned hearers not to answer a call to the altar unless they were coming under the definition of the call.

Form and Life

Bresee resisted architectural and liturgical features that put "form" ahead of "life," writing that "worldly members" might "try to ease their souls . . . with a worship made up more largely of dignity and liturgy," but "the really Christian people want something different: What they want is the real thing—salvation through the blood of the Lamb, by the power of the Holy Ghost. If a church does not have that, it matters little to earnest men what it has or has not—it does not meet human need."

Bresee's retort did not arise from ignorance of the liturgy. He complained that Episcopalians and Methodists did not take their own liturgy seriously enough. He mentioned two prayers in the liturgies of both churches. One was from the baptism liturgy: "Grant that all carnal affections may die in them, and that all things belonging to the Spirit may live and grow in them. Grant that they may have power and strength to have victory, and to triumph against the devil, the world, and the flesh." The other was the Collect for Purity at the beginning of the Order for Holy Communion: "Almighty God, unto whom all hearts are open, all desires known, and from whom no secrets are hid; Cleanse the thoughts of our hearts by the inspiration of thy Holy Spirit, that we may perfectly love thee, and worthily magnify thy holy Name; through Christ our Lord." Why complain, Bresee asked, if the Nazarenes claim the experience of a pure heart for which Episcopalians and Methodists pray?

Bresee linked formalism to deplorable ethics. Some who frequented fashionable churches were found the rest of the week at "saloons, hotel-bars, liquor-laden tables" and "the infamous ball play on the Sabbath." In 1903, preaching on Isa. 4:2-6, Bresee said:

Without holiness and the presence of him who dwells only in holy hearts, the church is soon a conquered church driveling for show; a beggar holding out its dirty hand for the world's pittance; or a ballet girl dancing and singing for the world's amusement and pay; or a blind old Samson grinding at the mill—brought out occasionally for the amusement of the Philistines. God's holy people are neither players for the world's amusement, nor caterers to the world's taste.

Worship

Bresee had little musical ability. He would strike up a hymn at no particular pitch, counting on others to bring it into usable range. He knew that better musicians than he were needed. The pianists, organists, and song leaders were to help the service, but not as entertainers.

In the Nazarene movement's early weeks, Bresee opposed paying the pianist. Better heads soon prevailed, but the pay was never adequate. Vocalists often stimulated the congregation to shouts of praise, but Bresee was wary of praise directed toward the singers. On one occasion, a guest who was to sing a solo before the sermon sat next to Bresee on the platform. She leaned over and apologized for needing to slip out before the sermon for another appointment. Bresee responded that the sermon was integral to the service; if she could not be there for it, she could not sing. She was sent on her way. Bresee said when dedicating the new church building at Sixth and Wall, "We studiously avoid performers." The gospel's very heart was at stake. Worship was an expression of lives transformed by God, or it was mere performance.

Bresee grew up with the Methodist hymnal of 1849, solid with Wesley hymns and other Protestant classics. He saw in the Wesley hymns a cry for help that needed to be enriched with songs of victory. He gave examples: "Since my eyes were fixed on Jesus," by Mary

James, and "How oft in holy converse," by Henrietta Blair. Los Angeles First Church used gospel songbooks, but when *Waves of Glory* was published in 1905, the classic tradition was not lost. One hundred twenty-four of the 308 songs were "standard hymns," of which 40 were by Charles Wesley.

Bresee gave particular attention to the offering. He wanted no public disclosure of the amount particular members gave. Bresee laid financial needs before the congregation. The offering often was taken by a procession of the whole congregation to a table at the front of the church, where gifts were laid on the table.

The Preachers

Bresee was Los Angeles First Church's principal preacher, but there were others. When he had an assistant pastor, Bresee preached once on Sunday, usually in the morning. He also preached at some weekday services. Other preaching was done by assistants, local preachers, laypeople, and visiting preachers. The latter were largely Methodists and Free Methodists, like C. J. Fowler, the National Holiness Association president, who conducted the congregation's first revival meeting.

Sometimes Bresee reached across the usual lines for his preacher. Augustus Prichard, pastor of First Presbyterian Church in Los Angeles, preached one Sunday evening. Bishop Coleman, a Free Methodist, was another guest. In 1903, when the Presbyterian General Assembly met in Los Angeles, Bresee requested someone from that body to preach at First Church on the evening of "the Anniversary of Pentecost." The Presbyterians sent James H. Hoadly, D.D., of New York City. Bresee commented afterward: "He seems to carry with him a joyous sense of the privilege he has of telling men the way of eternal life. We should be glad to hear him again." There was a ten-day revival meeting with "Bro. Nicols, Sisters Palmer and Smoots."

This "trio of colored evangelists . . . closed the special ten days meetings at the First Church on Sunday night. They are very sweet spirits and anointed workers. . . . Their teaching was very clear and scriptural." The congregation was exposed to a wide and constantly changing battery of preachers.

Attire

Bresee typically wore a black suit, a white shirt with a wing collar, and a black bow tie—the usual attire of Protestant clergy. He quoted a writer who stated that ministerial attire "should give the simple impression of a man and not a man of the world or of a follower of fashion. The less he is noticeable by his dress the better. He need not attract too much attention even by its simplicity. Simplicity which is on exhibition ceases to be simple and becomes a pose. . . . I should prefer that you be recognized by your temperament, which should be at once serious and kindly."

Similarly Bresee wrote: "We do not deem it necessary for women to publish their modesty by excessive expressions of it on their faces, but a modest air that would not call attention to themselves. . . . adornment is to be the incorruptible jewel of a meek and quiet spirit, to add in every way to the graces of womanhood." He added, these commands cannot be obeyed "without a sanctified heart. This matter of outward adornment is likely to be the signboard of the heart." Even being plain could become a matter of pride, manifested in faultfinding with others.

Church Architecture

Bresee scorned churches that prided themselves on fine buildings. Simple meeting houses of earlier days were giving way to neo-Gothic edifices for the urban middle classes. For Bresee, the only thing of importance was the Shekinah, the indwelling presence of

God among the people. In Hebrew literature, Shekinah referred to the direct presence or glory of God, as in the tabernacle, the temple, or in Jerusalem. It is the word underlying Rev. 7:15—"He that sitteth on the throne shall dwell among them."

The appeal to spiritual glory amid outward simplicity fit the early Nazarene meeting places—the two rented halls and the "tabernacle." But when the tabernacle, or Glory Barn, was no longer adequate, a new permanent church building was planned. Bresee expected it to be larger but still simple. Building codes, however, required a structure more costly and fine than Bresee's early ideas. The outcome was a building that rivaled the buildings of the "old-line" churches of Los Angeles, and Bresee was caught up in another impressive building project.

A large frame building like Pasadena's Methodist Tabernacle would have satisfied Bresee, but the fire code called for a building of "bricks, stone, and iron," doubling the building's cost. It was outwardly "churchly," with neo-Gothic embellishments reminiscent of Bresee's new church in Red Oak, Iowa. Before the interior was finished, the congregation moved furnishings from the Glory Barn and then marched through the streets to their new home at Sixth and Wall on Friday night, March 20, 1903. They set out from the old building singing, "Hallelujah! Amen!" led by "drums and other musical instruments." Bresee estimated that ten thousand people watched the march, and that twenty-five hundred packed the building for the opening service. The streets outside were jammed with people after the interior was filled.

It was dedicated the following Sunday. Bresee, the veteran "dedicator," preached from 2 Chron. 6:18, which told of the dedication of Solomon's temple. Bresee noted that the temple embodied not only cedars of Lebanon, gold, and silver but also "very much of the past." The "Divine providences of days gone by were through and through the temple." Solomon's people gathered, surrounded by a magnificent embodiment of God's faithfulness across the years.

Bresee asked his congregation the same question that for Solomon was "the all-absorbing question: Will God in very deed dwell with men on the earth?" Then he declared: "Today this observance will amount to little unless God answers by fire. If Christ be not glorified, then all is vain. I want to say that the same blessed glorious purpose is here this morning, that God may dwell in your hearts." He added: "In building this church we have provided for the multitude—a great multitude—to hear the Word of life and sit down at the table of Love Divine . . . We have no hired performers, either on instruments or in song. We studiously avoid performers. We seek no attraction, we want no attraction; by the grace of God we will have no attraction but the salvation of Jesus Christ." Later the congregation filed past the altar with "songs of triumph," laying their gifts on tables placed there.

The *Nazarene Messenger*

Early Los Angeles Nazarenes advertised with news releases and handbills. By 1897 they had a monthly paper called *The Nazarene*, edited by Bresee and Widney. At first it was a four-page paper. It carried advertisements for attorneys, marketers, trade people, and professionals including Dr. Paul Bresee, the Kregelo and Bresee funeral home, and the "Prohibition Grocery Store." It had devotional articles and contained news of the Nazarene churches in Oakland and Berkeley.

The paper became larger and more diverse. It became a weekly in July 1899. Lucy Knott wrote weekly Sunday school lessons. Alice Baldwin wrote a column for "Our Boys and Girls." There were reports from the Tuesday holiness meetings, and special features, such as a church history series. Articles and sermons frequently referred to earlier Christians—Polycarp, Irenaeus, Tauler, Luther, Calvin, Knox, the Wesleys, John Fletcher, Richard Watson, and Adam Clarke, conveying continuity with historic Christianity.

The name changed to the *Nazarene Messenger* in July 1900. It continued until 1912, when the *Herald of Holiness* was inaugurated in Kansas City, Missouri. The *Nazarene Messenger*'s broad coverage attracted readers from coast to coast. There was a running commentary on Methodism. Inspirational items extracted from Methodist periodicals were often followed by Bresee's comments. Other Protestant denominations came under his review, including Episcopalians, but he had little comment on Roman Catholics and Jews, nor much polemic against Calvinism. Bresee's primary quarrels were with Methodists for failing to live up to their mission to "spread Scriptural holiness." Calvinists were not expected to attain such high goals. Bresee commented on national politics, especially the liquor trade. President McKinley was criticized for not closing saloons, the more so since he was a Republican.

The paper resembled Methodist and other denominational papers of the time. Its growing national readership paved the way for the Los Angeles church to become a broadly based denomination. A reader in Hiawatha, Kansas, for example, joined the Los Angeles congregation by mail and sent her testimony from time to time. Bresee placed her picture on the pulpit when he publicly read her reports. Branch missions and new congregations sprang up in southern California and the San Francisco Bay area. The paper covered their news, too, and later the work in the Midwest. As merger with other denominations in the South and Northeast grew likely, still wider concerns and clientele resulted.

The paper's broadening scope brought new advertisers selling manufactured goods, patent medicines, and food. Some ads were pro coffee; others were anti-coffee. One ad offered stock in the Rio

Michol Rubber Plantation Company. An ad for O'Sullivan heels read: "Joy to the world, relief has come!" Railroads advertised excursions to southern California beaches and invited Easterners to California, using drawings of people in the voluminous bathing dress of the time. Swimming in the surf was promoted as good exercise. The Pasadena Rose Parade was promoted, along with the football game. Evidently criticized, Bresee defended the legitimacy of advertising "a proper business in a religious paper" one week. The next issue promoted Terminal Island as "The Ideal Beach . . . sheltered from the raw west winds and heavy seas, which makes a dip in the surf a real delight at all times of the year."

As merger with the Southern-based Holiness Church of Christ approached, commercial advertising ended, except from Christian schools and publishers. The final commercial ads were for real estate, honey, professional services, custom-made laundry and bakery wagons, and "the Clover Leaf Vibrator." An editorial announced the new policy: "We have decided to comply with the request of a portion of our constituency who are opposed to commercial advertising. . . . We do this for the best interest of the cause."

The *Nazarene Messenger* was an extension of Bresee's person and ministry. It expressed his earliest intentions for a holiness church in Los Angeles, and it increasingly reflected the adjustments and compromises he was willing to make to see his local church placed within a larger denomination spanning the continent and reaching into other lands. After the Nazarenes merged with other holiness denominations in 1907 and 1908, the new Pentecostal Church of the Nazarene had three denominational papers, each published in a different region of the United States, until 1912. When it ceased publication, Maria Bresee wrote a friend: "We feel bereft almost that we will not have the *Messenger* but we felt that the *Herald* will take high rank and meet the needs of all the people more fully than our own dear paper did." Bresee was relinquishing power to a movement that would outlast his life, if not his vision.

A University

In the midst of Bresee's many responsibilities, a church-sponsored college emerged in Los Angeles. Some laypeople, hoping to steer the Holiness Movement between the extremes of formalism and fanaticism, began planning a training school for Christian workers, and six women formed a Bible College Prayer Circle. C. W. Ruth presented their concerns to Bresee, and the women joined First Church in 1901.

Bresee was reluctant. His experiences with Simpson College and the University of Southern California made him cautious about a new venture with only one congregation to back it. Nevertheless, on July 28, 1902, a board of trustees was organized with Bresee as its president. The school opened in September. It was named Pacific Bible College after Bresee rejected the suggestion of naming it for him.

Bresee was president, and C. W. Ruth was vice president. Bresee agreed to teach, but the administrator was Mary Hill, a former missionary in China. It was a setback when she returned suddenly to China in 1904, taking a number of students with her.

Leora Maris became the new principal, and most of the faculty were women. Bresee taught a course on Isaiah, the book he regarded as a gold mine of truth concerning God's holiness. Teachers donated their time. After Ruth left to return to full-time evangelism, C. V. La Fontaine became vice president and a teacher in 1904.

The dream of a larger school and campus seemed realized in 1906, when Jackson Deets, a Nazarene businessman, offered thirty thousand dollars. The first ten thousand dollars were to buy a seven-acre site. Bresee and others began to think of a "university." Grandiose plans were laid, and lots surrounding the school were to be sold. This familiar pattern had been used at Simpson Centenary College and the University of Southern California. Deets Pacific Bible College was to be the first department of a larger Nazarene university.

The negotiations between the college board and the donors have been told elsewhere, most clearly in Ronald B. Kirkemo's *For Zion's Sake: The History of Pasadena/Point Loma College* (San Diego: Point Loma Press, 1992). Money was lacking, arrangements and promises fell by the wayside, and there were misunderstandings. By 1907 it was not clear that the college could remain open. The burden fell upon the official board of Los Angeles First Church. For a time, the boards governing college and congregation were interlocking. The congregation assumed the college's operating expenses and kept its eyes on the school's internal work.

Bresee was increasingly burdened with duties and attempted several times to resign the pastorate. Each time, the church board persuaded him to remain. Ruth lightened the burden as assistant pastor (1901-3), followed by La Fontaine (1904-7), Bresee's cousin-once-removed and former pastor of South Chicago Methodist Episcopal Church. Bresee's third assistant pastor, A. L. Whitcomb, a Free Methodist, was a poor fit and actually led a schism, taking fifty members from First Church. Bresee felt deeply betrayed by Whitcomb and those who left with him and opposed their request to enter the district as a Nazarene congregation. In 1910, however, district superintendent John Goodwin admitted them despite Bresee's objections.

College affairs remained unsettled. Even the school's denominational affiliation was uncertain for a time. Eventually, though, it moved to Pasadena and became known as Nazarene University. The new campus was financed in part by subdividing and selling much of it for home sites. Bresee bought several of them. He remained First Church pastor and university president until 1911, when he resigned both offices, but he was heavily involved in college affairs until his death in 1915.

FIFTEEN

A UNITING CHURCH

❧

Bresee held the offices of pastor and general superintendent. He edited the *Nazarene Messenger*, wrote many of its editorials, and often published his Sunday sermon. He preached at conferences and camp meetings across America and became president of a new college. Later, after he resigned his pastorate and there were other general superintendents, it was still difficult to relinquish earlier burdens.

New churches sprang up in Los Angeles, Berkeley, and Oakland. Emma Stine Colborn wanted a Nazarene church in Seattle, where Bresee's former Iowa friend, H. D. Brown, was a Methodist pastor. By 1903 Bresee had visited Salt Lake City, where I. G. Martin and C. W. Ruth had opened a church, and Boise, Idaho, where Englishman Robert Pierce labored. He also visited Omaha, Nebraska; Maples Mills, Illinois; and Spokane, Washington.

H. D. Brown left Seattle's Battery Street Methodist Episcopal Church and in 1904 became superintendent of the Northwest District—the first Nazarene district. Prayer meetings were held in Brown's home, and Bresee preached in a revival in 1905. A group committed "to carry on the work," and Bresee organized a class under J. R. Amon, who, "with Bro. C. O. Bangs and Sister E. S. Colborn, were appointed an Executive Committee." Brown and Mrs.

Colborn were friends from Bresee's Methodist days. Bangs, from Norway, had found the Nazarene meetings to be more of a "family church" than the Salvation Army, whose work he once led in the logging town of Roslyn, Washington. He and his Swiss bride, Méry Dupertuis, had made Bresee's Los Angeles church a destination goal on their honeymoon earlier that year. Bresee built on old friendships and developed new ones to expand the denomination.

In Spokane, Elsie Wallace led the John Three Sixteen Mission. It became a Nazarene church after C. W. Ruth conducted a revival in 1902. Bresee visited and ordained Mrs. Wallace. She was the first woman whom he ordained an elder. The next year, he ordained Lucy Knott in Los Angeles.

Bresee's travels increased. He preached in Kansas. He organized a fast-growing church in Chicago in 1904. Congregations in Illinois and Indiana gave Nazarenes a presence in the Midwest, and an international dimension was added when the church adopted missionary work in Calcutta, India, in 1906. Bresee ordained the founder of the Calcutta work, Mrs. Sukhoda Banerjee, and her son-in-law, Mr. Biswas.

Mergers

The emergence of the Pentecostal Church of the Nazarene as a national and international denomination is told elsewhere. E. A. Girvin gave an eyewitness account in his biography of Bresee. Timothy L. Smith gives a modern narrative and analysis in *Called unto Holiness* (1962) as does *Our Watchword and Song: The Centennial History of the Church of the Nazarene* (2009). Our focus is narrower. We are occupied with Bresee and those things that tested his powers and faith in his last years of life.

Bresee worked with other holiness leaders across the country through the National Holiness Association. C. W. Ruth, Bresee's associate pastor (1901-3) and assistant general superintendent (1901-

7), retained lifelong NHA ties and showed Bresee the possibilities of cooperation and union with other groups.

The Association of Pentecostal Churches of America resulted from an earlier merger of holiness churches in the New England and Mid-Atlantic states. The New England branch stemmed from a congregation founded in Providence, Rhode Island, in 1887. By 1905, the Church of the Nazarene had contact with the Easterners through John Goodwin and Robert Pierce, former participants in the New England Holiness Movement, who had moved west and become Nazarene pastors. C. W. Ruth preached regularly in the East, and Bresee did so occasionally.

Ruth addressed the 1906 annual meeting of the Association of Pentecostal Churches. That autumn, three Eastern leaders visited Nazarene churches in Chicago, Spokane, Seattle, San Francisco, and Los Angeles, meeting Bresee and other Nazarene leaders. In April 1907, Bresee, Brown, and Girvin visited Brooklyn, New York, to negotiate a merger of the denominations. The chief obstacle was polity. The Easterners were congregational in government, while the Nazarenes had a strong superintendency and held property in the general church's name.

The two denominations met in joint assembly in Chicago, October 10-17, 1907. Bresee presented a comprehensive report similar to the episcopal address at the Methodist General Conference. A commission had formulated the basis of union, and final details were agreed upon in committees and plenary sessions. Bresee presided over sessions marked by candor, rejoicing, and emotion. Hard decisions were made. The East accepted superintendency. The General Assembly also called for two general superintendents. Local churches would call their pastors, subject to the district superintendent's approval. Existing Eastern churches would retain control of their property, but all former Nazarene churches, and all churches organized after the assembly, would have a deed restriction placed on their property. Otherwise, little differed from the Church of the Nazarene's previous *Manual*.

Bresee was reelected general superintendent by acclamation, and Hiram F. Reynolds was elected by ballot as his colleague. No provision was made for salaries. Bresee's income came from his pastorate. Reynolds was elected missionary secretary and derived salary from that office.

Isaiah Reid, a venerable NHA leader, marveled at the new unity achieved: "Here meet and mingle in blessed unity and fellowship a multitude of people once divided in many ways but now merged into a harmonized body of saints."

The names of the two parent churches were combined into Pentecostal Church of the Nazarene. This was the tenth general meeting for both churches, but that numbering was dropped. The Chicago meeting became the First General Assembly of the Pentecostal Church of the Nazarene.

Fraternal delegates attended from other holiness churches. Horace Trumbauer, from the Pennsylvania Conference of the Holiness Christian Church, sat with the fourteen-member union commission. His participation paved the way for the Pennsylvania Conference (but not its sister Indiana Conference) to join the new denomination in September 1908.

The other visitors were seven delegates from the Holiness Church of Christ, created in 1904 by merging two holiness groups active in Texas, Arkansas, Tennessee, and Oklahoma, with new congregations in Georgia, Florida, and Alabama. The Southerners could not take binding action on their denomination's behalf, so a second union assembly was required to embrace this group. Bresee faced different issues in negotiating with the Holiness Church of Christ. Timothy Smith states that "the issue of law versus Christian charity was to dominate efforts to unite North and South." At issue were the second coming of Christ, divine healing, lodge membership, the wearing of gold, short sleeves on girls' dresses, and tobacco use. The first two issues were removed from controversy in 1907 by the adoption in Chicago of moderating articles of faith. The Church of the Nazarene had handled other issues, like tobacco use, under "Special Advices."

Bresee made a foray into Texas in April 1908, conducting revival services at Texas Holiness University near Greenville. On April 7 he organized a local independent church into a Pentecostal Nazarene congregation, appointing Emily Ellyson, wife of the college president, as pastor. This gave the Pentecostal Nazarenes a small foothold in the South before the Pilot Point assembly.

The Second General Assembly convened at Pilot Point, Texas, on October 8, 1908. The two sides seemed far apart on the issue of "law versus charity." Bresee's emphasis, says Timothy Smith, "was still upon the discipline of the Spirit. He especially resisted enforcement of the strictures on women's dress in 1 Timothy 2:9 and 1 Peter 3:3. Easterners generally seem to have shared this position. But the Holiness Church of Christ had long forbade by rules what others had simply advised their people to shun." H. D. Brown found the South's apparent legalism hard to take, once calling out to Bresee, "Mr. Chairman, let them go." Bresee's famous answer was irenic: "We can't let them go, Brother Brown; they are our own folks." Compromises were reached. Some "advices" became "rules." Bresee and Reynolds were reelected as general superintendents, and E. P. Ellyson was elected as the third.

Bresee played the statesman. He spoke of the Holiness Movement as providential, with confluent streams coming from east, west, and south. The "happy union of the East and West" had been followed by "this confluence of the South; turning us all like the rivers of the south; pouring much of the holiness movement into an organic whole." Northerners L. Milton Williams and I. G. Martin wrote some doggerel titled "The Battle Hymn of the Assembly" and had the wit to set it to the tune of "Dixie."

The union of 1908 achieved something far more difficult than that of 1907: it united North and South. The delegates realized their achievement, and when the merger was effected by a unanimous vote, Northerners and Southerners embraced each other in fervent rejoicing.

It is a notable event in American church history, usually ignored by historians. Most major American denominations were still divided by the Civil War. Methodists did not reunite until 1939. Presbyterians reunited in 1983 at the cost of large defections. Baptists have not reunited and perhaps never will. Bresee called these mergers "this answering of the Lord's prayer that they may be one."

Mergers were discussed with other groups, including the Pentecostal Mission. The Pentecostal Alliance formed in Nashville in 1898, under J. O. McClurkan, a Cumberland Presbyterian. It was not intended as a new denomination and cooperated with the Christian and Missionary Alliance in education and missions. But the Christian and Missionary Alliance became increasingly denominational, and the Pentecostal Alliance assumed a more denominational character of its own and took the name "Pentecostal Mission" in 1901.

McClurkan and Bresee corresponded in 1907. On January 1, McClurkan wrote of his hope for a movement that would "embrace the Pentecostal people of different temperaments and denominational bias." He recognized the need "to form congregations" and "follow up the work systematically." The Church of the Nazarene, he said, was "nearer our ideal" than "any other which we know, and yet there may be difficulties." Some were easily overcome. The Nazarene name was acceptable to McClurkan, while Nazarenes would welcome the Pentecostal Mission's extensive missionary work.

McClurkan noted that "the vast majority of our people are Arminian in their views," but he wanted a "broader basis of doctrinal agreement" than Arminianism or Calvinism alone could provide, one with "a little more emphasis being put on Grace," which he believed was being neglected in favor of works. McClurkan called, also, for greater emphasis on "the perfecting of character" as a process following the act of consecration and faith by which the believer enters the sanctified life.

On polity, he acknowledged that "independentism" harbored dangers unless accompanied by organization "on a broad scriptural basis." McClurkan did not raise the issue of dispensational premillennialism, but the Pentecostal Mission embraced it.

Bresee's letter of August 1 went to the issues, including dispensationalism:

> A doctrinal basis of necessary belief should be very simple and embrace what is essential to holiness. All not essential to holiness should be relegated to personal liberty. . . . We have acted upon the conviction that the grand dispensational truth, that which makes us a dispensation, is that Jesus Christ baptizes believers with the Holy Spirit, sanctifying and empowering them. Our unity is in the simplicity of necessary belief and the perfect liberty in reference to all other truth.

Bresee addressed polity, saying that "undenominational work" would "pass away soon. Those who seek wide and lasting results must organize."

Pentecostal Mission delegates attended the general assemblies in Chicago and Pilot Point. Pentecostal Nazarenes were invited to hold their third General Assembly in Nashville in 1911 and accepted. Pentecostal Mission leaders observed the General Assembly struggle with the issue of three regional church papers. The decision to combine them into *Herald of Holiness* strengthened the church's ties to the Southeast after B. F. Haynes of Tennessee was named its editor. But McClurkan was ambivalent about merger until just before his death in 1914. After a long courtship, the Pentecostal Mission united with the Pentecostal Church of the Nazarene on April 15, 1915. Bresee played a substantive role in effecting the union.

The church unions altered Bresee's position, making him one of three general superintendents. The church was also changing—united, now, from west, east, and south. Individuals, congregations, and small movements joined it. Bresee was involved in some, but not all, negotiations. District superintendents also played primary roles. Bresee sought to bring in a group from Colorado but failed.

Another accession occurred at the Chicago Central District's 1912 assembly, where Bresee presided. The district accepted Illinois Holiness University. Two years later, Bresee set foot on its campus at Olivet, Illinois, when he conducted the 1914 assembly. On this occasion, "Dr. Bresee made a stirring address, pointing out many of the possibilities of this institution" at an outdoor rally that promoted the sale of lots platted around the school.

The mergers in 1915 greatly extended the Pentecostal Church of the Nazarene's range. In addition to the Pentecostal Mission, a merger was effected with the Pentecostal Church of Scotland. Bresee had little direct role in this one. The key roles were played by George Sharpe of Scotland, Olive Winchester, Hiram Reynolds, and Edward F. Walker, who succeeded Ellyson as general superintendent in 1911. The union was finalized at the 1915 General Assembly in Kansas City.

Shared Leadership

Leadership of the Pentecostal Church of the Nazarene was passing into other hands. At the 1908 union, Bresee was nearly seventy. Unlike Methodist bishops, he was reelected at each General Assembly, but like them he assumed the office was his for life.

A team relationship was necessary to guide the denomination as it expanded and added new districts. In 1912 Bresee presided over district assemblies in the Rocky Mountains, the Dakotas, the Midwest, and the South. In 1914 he crisscrossed the country to preside in New Jersey, New York, Rhode Island, Pennsylvania, Washington State, California, Kansas, Nebraska, Illinois, Iowa, Arkansas, Missouri, and Oklahoma—in that order. Furthermore, his failing health led him to authorize W. C. Wilson to preside in his stead at assemblies in the Southeast.

General superintendents maintained constant communication by mail and telegraph. The Bresee-Reynolds correspondence reflects their spirit and methods. Their letters are marked by the formality and courtesy characteristic of the era, but also by heartfelt Christian devotion, personal respect, and affection. Reynolds's letters were usually addressed to "P. F. Bresee, D.D.," or "Rev. P. F. Bresee," with such salutations as "My very dear brother" or "My Dear Brother in Christ, Greetings in Jesus." One began, "Dear Brother Dr. Bresee: God bless you!" Bresee addressed Reynolds with a similar blend of formality and Christian warmth: "My Dear Brother Reynolds."

Their letters dealt with everything from travel and assembly schedules to personnel matters and pastoral supply. They conferred and sought legal opinions on the ownership of church properties. There were problems with the incorporation of churches, the interpretation of the property ownership agreement of 1907, and the raising and handling of money at local, district, and national levels.

They received no salaries for their office, yet both men showed far more concern about the poverty of the churches. What should they do, for example, about the extreme poverty of the members of the Pentecostal Church of Scotland? Illness was a recurring topic. Bresee was often ill; Mrs. Reynolds had a serious heart problem. In instances of uncertainty due to health or communication, one ceded to the other authority to act without further consultation.

Some of their decisions set precedents. One case turned on a question of ordination. The Second General Assembly had elected Leighton S. Tracy to elder's orders, but Tracy was a missionary in India. There were no funds to bring him to the United States or to send a superintendent to India, yet both men believed that Tracy should be ordained by the laying on of hands by an elder or elders previously ordained by the laying on of hands.

Bresee suggested that they ask a Methodist Episcopal bishop in India to ordain Tracy as a courtesy to the Nazarenes. Reynolds, however, remembered that there were missionaries in India sent by the Holiness Church of Christ, now part of the Pentecostal Church of the Nazarene. Were they ordained? Reynolds inquired of Rev. Mrs. E. J. Sheeks, the district secretary in Arkansas. She reported that Mr. and Mrs. L. A. Campbell had been ordained by the Holiness Church of Christ on June 1, 1907. Reynolds and Bresee were satisfied and instructed Campbell to ordain Tracy on the basis of the General Assembly action and the authority delegated to him by the general superintendents. That ordination service brought the missionaries in India from the three Nazarene parent bodies together for their first joint assembly. Bresee willingly accepted actions proposed by his younger colleague.

SIXTEEN

LAST DAYS

❧

Private Life

What of Bresee's private life? Ernest earned his degree at Simpson Centenary College in Iowa and then entered into business in Los Angeles with Phineas W. and Melvin. They began as lumber merchants manufacturing coffins and formed Bresee Brothers' Mortuary in 1892. Melvin, Ernest, and Phineas W. were lifelong Methodists. Melvin and Phineas were members of Simpson Tabernacle for a time. Simpson later merged with Wilshire Methodist Church, where Melvin donated a stained-glass window. The brothers were often mentioned on the newspaper's society page.

Bertha Bresee married Pasadena dentist John Parker. She taught Sunday school during her father's Pasadena pastorate, and one pupil later became her pastor there. On a European trip in 1906, the Parkers' little daughter Lillian died in Belgium and was buried there. Dr. Parker made dentures for his father-in-law in 1911.

Paul Bresee, a physician, married Ada Glidden. Their son was Horace Hebbard Bresee. Ada was a devoted Nazarene leader and a cofounder of the Woman's Missionary Society, now Nazarene Missions International. As district secretary for Southern California from 1917 to 1946, she signed the credentials of many ordinands. Susan Bresee lived with Paul and Ada until 1927, when she married widower C. J. Kinne. Fred Cowley died in Bakersfield, California, in 1908, leaving no survivors.

Phineas and Maria lived in parsonages during his Methodist ministry, but in late 1894 they made their home in a private residence, subsequently moving twice. In 1898 they moved in with Paul and Ada. Paul's medical practice was also located in the home. Phineas and Maria, and Bertha and Sue until their marriages, remained in the Paul and Ada Bresee home. The household's other member was young Horace, a boy with beautiful blond curls and (so he later claimed) an imperious manner. Horace was the object of parental doting and too much public attention. He told the author how his grandfather, while writing letters and sermons, chided him for the noise he made. The home on Santee Street was a large Victorian house surrounded by porches. It was in a spacious suburb with wide lawns and a coach house, near downtown Los Angeles.

Sue Bresee's diaries reflect the family's life. The household was busy. "Mattie" was the maid. In 1909, the family wanted to eat in the kitchen and have Mattie sit with them; she refused, so the family ate in the dining room. There were constant guests, especially for meals. Sue recorded visits by E. F. Walker, C. V. La Fontaine, John Goodwin, Cora Snyder, C. E. McKee, and "Mr. Coleman"; Nancy Radford, a deaconess; Mr. Fuller and Mr. Chenault, who were going to Japan; Fred Epperson, a frequent visitor; Mr. and Mrs. Leslie Gay; and Sue's brothers, among others. In 1915, the visitors included H. Orton Wiley; Earl Wilde, song leader at Los Angeles First Church; Professor A. J. Ramsay; the Willises, who drove Bresee family members home from church; the Nazarene University faculty on April 4; and Mr. and Mrs. John Goodwin. E. A. Girvin was a frequent visitor. Sue recorded one remarkable Sunday: "No one came home with us for dinner."

Sue recorded vignettes of the church. "Mr. Walker preached an hour. It was so cold Grace and I came down out of the choir when he was half through." That evening, "Mr. W. preached an hour again and not a great sermon." On another Sunday, "Mr. Walker preached a good sermon—had a fine crowd." She complained in 1915 that her parents "think we should be there in all meetings." Once she wrote: "[C. E.] Cornell preached on healing, had healing service. Did not get any help from the service." After another service she wrote: "Cornell preached on the second coming, pre & post. I wish Cornell would put more time on his sermons." "Mrs. C. had quite a shout." Then this: "Cornell didn't preach much but jumped around some at the altar." For Sue, her father's successor would never measure up. One Sunday in 1909, "Prof. Ramsay preached for us this morning. A fine sermon." At a prayer meeting, "Had Selectman [sic] from M.E. Church give us a talk on John Wes[ley]." That was Charles C. Selecman, later a bishop. At another service, "Mr. Lillenas played organ."

Bresee preached from his old pulpit from time to time. In 1909, Sue noted: "Papa . . . preached fine—about 40 minutes." Later that year: "I went to prayer meeting with Papa. Papa had charge and it seemed like old times. Many spoke of it. We ended up with a march. Mr. W. and Mrs. Lynch wouldn't march." Evidently not everyone favored the old exuberance! In 1915 she reports: "Cora [Snyder] and I went out to hear Papa preach. It was fine and so different from anything I ever heard him preach before. . . . The way we were packed reminded me of the old tabernacle days." Another Sunday, "Papa had charge . . . Papa had them all come around the altar after the sacrament and sing, pray, and praise the Lord."

The Bresees were constantly concerned about the college. A rift with Seth C. Rees was looming. Old-time Nazarene Lily Bothwell had a "vision" that Rees would soon leave Pasadena. Sue wrote: "I hope Mrs. Bothwell's vision proves true." Rees had charged Professor A. J.

Ramsay with Calvinist leanings and wanted Fred Epperson removed from the ministry. The Bresees supported both men, and the Eppersons often visited their home. Bresee insisted on fair play. No one was to be dismissed based on rumors and arbitrary administration.

Home was not barricaded against Bresee's duties. Conferences, faculty meetings, and board meetings were held there. He wrote out his sermons there. In the last year of life, with his health failing, Bresee still made time for his family. In March 1915 Sue wrote, "Papa has been reading us 'The Return of Pollyana.' It is fine."

The Last Assembly

In 1908 Bresee was nearly seventy. His heart troubled him, but his responsibilities did not diminish. Maria often traveled with him. Her letters to Emma Colborn report a variety of illnesses, and she was deeply concerned as the 1915 General Assembly in Kansas City approached. Sue Bresee's diary gives an account of the trip. Delegates and friends from Southern California left Los Angeles by train on September 22. Friends bid them farewell, providing eight boxes of fruit, tomatoes, fried chicken, candy, and cookies.

The group rode together in one car. The Bresee family group included Phineas, Maria, Sue, and Ada. The ministerial delegates included district superintendent Howard Eckel, Seth and Freda Rees, Bud Robinson, C. E. Cornell, H. Orton Wiley, C. W. Ruth, A. M. Bowes, and John Goodwin. The lay delegates included Ada Bresee, Mr. and Mrs. Leslie Gay, Sally Robinson, Mrs. C. E. Cornell, and D. H. Ely. There were nearly thirty Nazarene passengers in all.

On the first day Sue wrote: "Had family worship this day." At times they sang and prayed. Two delegates testified, and passengers came from other cars to observe. "All visit around a good deal," Sue wrote, but "Rees stays to himself or does not come to see Papa much, did for about three minutes today but seemed to be in a rush to get away. She [Freda Rees] is very nice, though."

On September 23 Sue wrote: "Papa is feeling the altitude and very tired." The next day: "Papa had a hard night and could hardly breathe going over the highest place." Their trip, by way of Salt Lake City and Cheyenne, Wyoming, reached elevations exceeding seven thousand feet, and several passengers were distressed. There was coal dust and smoke from the locomotive. "Our white skirts looked awful."

In Cheyenne, Sue and others climbed to the dome of the new state capitol. At Denver the Bresees and others detoured to Colorado Springs, visiting the Garden of the Gods, the Cave of the Winds, and Seven Falls. Finally they made the long run across Kansas to Kansas City.

Bresee was seriously ill, and Ada wired Paul to come at once and attend his father. Maria recounted the events to Emma Colborn: "How anxious he was to be at that assembly. . . . when he took the chair and presided, he seemed so strong that no one realized that he was so sick, so near the heavenly home." Bresee read the general superintendent's report, which he had written and the others had approved. The reading took forty-five minutes. That afternoon he preached on Isa. 53 for the Communion service. He was unable to preach as scheduled that evening and missed some other assembly sessions.

He was reelected as a general superintendent, receiving 210 of 220 ballots cast, yet it was apparent to all that he would not serve out his term. Warm expressions of affection and respect were made. The oldest representatives of the united holiness churches, summoned by William Howard Hoople and led by Mary Lee Cagle, presented Bresee with a bouquet of seventy-seven red roses, one for each completed year of life, and a white rose for the unfinished year.

Dr. Paul Bresee tried relieving his pain with the common remedy in those days. Bresee probably was not told what it was, nor did he want to know. Horace always remembered that his granddad asked simply for "that stuff." At times, it impaired his ability.

Back in Los Angeles, Bresee called in friends and confidants for parting words and instructions. E. A. Girvin spent considerable time with him and included their conversations in his biography of Bresee. Bresee told Girvin: "The greatest blessing I have ever had is my wife." There was no reconciliation with Seth Rees, who continued his attacks on Fred Epperson, one of Bresee's protégés. Bresee also summoned H. Orton Wiley and exhorted him to "Stay by the college."

On November 4, Bresee's family gathered—Maria, Ernest, Phineas W., Paul, Melvin, Bertha, Susan, Ada, and Paul. Bresee prayed for each by name. He also dictated a last message to the Nazarenes:

My last message to all my people— Ministers and laymen—is that they seek until they have the conscious, abiding, manifesting experience that Jesus insists upon in these verses found in Matthew 5:43 to 46 inclusive; not in word only but in deed and in truth, so shall Jesus be glorified:

43. Ye have heard that it hath been said, Thou shalt love thy neighbour, and hate thine enemy.

44. But I say unto you, Love your enemies, bless them that curse you, do good to them that hate you, and pray for them which despitefully use you, and persecute you;

45. That ye may be the children of your Father which is in heaven: for he maketh his sun to rise on the evil and on the good, and sendeth rain on the just and on the unjust.

46. For if ye love them which love you, what reward have ye? do not even the publicans the same?

The end came on November 13. The memorial service was held three days later in the First Pentecostal Church of the Nazarene in Los Angeles. The participants were pastor C. E. Cornell, district superintendent Howard Eckel, Girvin, John Goodwin, Dean E. A.

Healey of the theological department of the University of Southern California, music professor William Jones of Nazarene University, and H. Orton Wiley. Memorial tributes poured in from many places.

The Methodists noted Bresee's passing. The *California Christian Advocate* reviewed Bresee's Methodist ministry and said: "Dr. Bresee was a very able preacher and especially effective as an evangelist. He was a man who was greatly admired and loved by a large personal following." A full-length portrait of the Bresees accompanied the article.

The Southern California District paid another tribute, perhaps unique in church history, that was indirect but touching. For several years Maria had been listed in district minutes under the category of "Evangelists not Elders." The district minutes for June 23, 1917, however, have a distinctive item: "On motion by Rev. Will H. Nerry, Mrs. P. F. Bresee was recommended for Elder's orders. The vote was unanimous, and the entire Assembly was touched with tender love and sympathy." The next day, "a very large audience gathered in the afternoon. A class of elders . . . were ordained. . . . This was a very spiritual and impressive service."

Maria Bresee accepted the action as a tribute to her late husband. She wrote Emma Stine Colborn in Seattle: "Sunday afternoon ordination and consecration of deaconesses service, and what do you think? The Assembly elected me to elders orders. It was such a surprise to me, for I had never thought of such a thing. I protested, but they so pressed it that I finally yielded and was ordained. . . . I take it as an honor to my precious husband."

She lived until March 13, 1920. The 1920 district minutes speaks of her as a "true helpmeet . . . a tower of strength to her husband . . . her life given to her children and the home . . . [she] exemplified the grace of entire sanctification." Her ordination was obliquely referenced: "Henceforth the name of this warrior will be absent from our roll, and we will miss her face at our annual gatherings."

WHO WAS BRESEE?

Bresee answered a call to preach when he was, as he put it, "only a boy." He preached for the next sixty years. He was occupied with many interests—marriage and family, church administration, business ventures, building campaigns, colleges, and fashioning a new church's structure and doctrine. Like a symphony conductor whose complex life focuses on the one point of standing before an orchestra and conducting great music, Bresee's complex life found fulfillment in one point—standing before the congregation and expounding the Word of life. His life found its unity in preaching.

A theological decision lay at the heart of Bresee's message. This decision was tied to the divine personality, rooted in the conviction that God's person is more than the divine attributes of omnipotence and omniscience. "What is God? God is holy love." Contact with God is contact with awesome holiness, and "we cannot trifle with holiness."

There are implications for the church: "Without holiness and the presence of him who dwells only in holy hearts, the church is soon a conquered church driveling for show; a beggar holding out its dirty hand for the world's pittance; or a ballet girl dancing and singing for the world's amusement and pay, or a blind old Samson grinding at the mill—brought out occasionally for the amusement of the Philistines. God's holy people are neither players for the world's amusement, nor caterers to the world's taste."

Sanctification was not optional for those seeking a "higher life." It was the very essence of Christian life. But why insist on sanctification as a "second blessing"? He did so because those who are encountered by the holiness of God in Jesus Christ are convicted of their guilt and seek forgiveness. Only this forgiveness clears the way for Christian holiness.

Bresee was neither a fundamentalist nor a modernist. In his view, Christ does more than die for our sins or live for our example. Christ touches the believer with the very holiness of God. Christ baptizes the believer, he often said, with the Holy Spirit. Rules of conduct and creeds are beside the point without "the transforming power of the Spirit of God."

Bresee was a man of his times. With contemporaries, he struggled over the slavery issue. He favored women's rights and, in the 1890s, ensured women's full equality in the Church of the Nazarene. He recognized the personal and social evils of alcohol but was too sanguine, perhaps, about prohibition's ultimate success. He consorted with the nabobs of the Gilded Age and found them wanting. He was a pastor to an emerging middle class.

Bresee was attuned spiritually to many deep human currents at the turn of the century. He understood the growing concern of religious thinkers to counter the mechanistic, reductionist skepticism that was an acid to Christian belief. He countered reductionism by preaching on the Spirit who gives life and hope. He used creeds and forms but placed his emphasis on the life-giving Spirit at work in human lives and history. When Bresee preached, deep called out to deep.

Bresee feared a doctrine of holiness that allowed one to claim to have "arrived." A contemporary alleged that Bresee, having felt that he was perfect, was compelled to start a new church. The charge missed its mark. For Bresee, transformation by holy love allows one—nay, *calls* one—to grow. He once said that the Old Testament is repressive, while the New Testament is liberating. He knew better: witness his love for Isaiah. But the point—though mistaken—was important because it exemplified the theme of freedom through divine grace threaded throughout Bresee's message.

Sanctification as freedom is no mere "blessing." It opens doors that are awesome. It is frightening to peer into the ever larger rooms behind them. The "blessing" is also a blessed burden.

This comes through clearly in a startling sermon of Bresee's. We have only his manuscript, with very little spelled out. There are suggestions, with a poignant cry at the end. It is reconstructed here, with Bresee's actual words in italics. The text is Ruth 2:19: "Where hast thou gleaned to day?"

Bresee talks about *where we glean today—the fields of literature, social life, meditation, worship. . . . We glean in the field of truth . . . industriously, humbly, affectionately.* But, he asks, *what is the wheat?*

And then, in bold letters scrawled across the center of the page, he abruptly puts the name:

"Gutenberg."

Why? Because the answer to the question about the wheat becomes easily distorted, and Bresee feels that Gutenberg bears some blame.

> *Reliance on printed matter has destroyed oral teaching, the dissemination of thought by the spoken word. Printing has formed a literary class looking to the making of books. Reliance on books does much to weaken the powers of memory, which is fatal to the orderly arrangement of thought.*

A large open space suddenly appears on the page of Bresee's manuscript. He is withdrawn, struggling to express what he wants to say about the wheat—about the truth we are to glean. Finally, he writes out the poignant cry of one who has glimpsed the holy God.

> *I wish sometimes I could preach with closed eyes. Could preach to you from the solitude of my own soul. Could tell the visions that sometimes come over me. But they are born in solitude, live in solitude, and will not come forth.*

❧APPENDIX☙

SELECTED CHRONOLOGY

cᗷᗩ

1838   Phineas Franklin Bresee born in Franklin, New York.

1850   P. P. Bresee family moves to Valley Farm, West Davenport, New York.

1856   Bresee professes conversion; delivers his first sermon.

1857   The Bresees move to farm west of Millersburg, Iowa. Bresee received on trial in Iowa Conference of Methodist Episcopal Church; appointed assistant on Marengo Circuit.

1859   Ordained a deacon by Bishop Matthew Simpson; elected as full member of conference; appointed to Pella.

1860   Marries Maria Hebbard in Davenport Center, New York; appointed to Grinnell Circuit.

1861   Ordained an elder by Bishop Levi Scott; appointed to Galesburg Circuit.

1862   Appointed to East Des Moines.

1864   Appointed presiding elder of the Winterset District, Des Moines Conference.

1866   Appointed to Chariton; struggles with doubt; reports entire sanctification.

1868   Appointed to Wesley Chapel, Des Moines.

1870   Appointed to Broadway Church, Council Bluffs.

1871   Elected delegate to General Conference.

1872   Attends General Conference in Brooklyn, New York.

1873   Appointed to Red Oak; builds new church facility.

1876   Appointed to Clarinda.

1879   Appointed to Creston; involved in promoting mining stock.

1880   Appointed to second term at Broadway Church, Council Bluffs.

1882   Appointed to start a new church in a proposed Council Bluffs subdivision; site flooded.

1883   Moves to California; transferred by Bishop Simpson to Southern California Conference; appointed by Bishop Henry Warren to Fort Street Church, Los Angeles.

1884   Defends Methodism against attacks by radical holiness people.

1886   Convenes a select committee to plan Simpson Tabernacle Methodist Episcopal Church in Los Angeles; appointed to First Church, Pasadena.

1887   Inaugurates the Christmas love feast, a gathering of holiness people, in Pasadena.

1888   Pasadena tabernacle built next to the church to accommodate crowds; Simpson Tabernacle attempts to get Bresee as pastor.

1890   Appointed to Asbury Church, Los Angeles.

1891   Elected to lead Southern California Conference delegation to General Conference; appointed presiding elder; holds revival meetings throughout southern California.

1892   Attends General Conference in Omaha; appointed to Simpson Tabernacle.

1893   Appointed to Boyle Heights Church, Los Angeles.

1894   Withdraws from Southern California Conference; with J. P. Widney, affiliates with Peniel Mission.

1895   Church of the Nazarene organized in Los Angeles with Bresee and Widney as conjoint pastors and general superintendents.

1898   Widney withdraws from Church of the Nazarene.

1907   Pentecostal Church of the Nazarene formed by union of Church of the Nazarene with Association of Pentecostal Churches of America.

1908   Holiness Church of Christ brought into united church.

1915   Bresee dies on November 13.

SELECTED BRESEE GENEALOGY

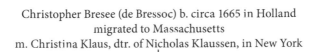

Christopher Bresee (de Bressoc) b. circa 1665 in Holland
migrated to Massachusetts
m. Christina Klaus, dtr. of Nicholas Klaussen, in New York

Nicholas Bresee (Bruzie), b. 1682
m. 1706 to Catarina (Catarijntje) Bont
Their children include

Christopher (Christoffel) Bresee (Bressee),
Andries Bresee b. June 15, 1707, in Albany, New York, died 1789
m. Nov. 11, 1737, to Agneta Rosman
Either Christopher or Andries was the father of John C. Bresee

John C. Bresee (Brazie, Brazee), b. 1739
m. Elizabeth Rosman (Rossman)

Jeremiah Bresee, d. 1827

Phineas Philips Bresee
m. Susan Brown

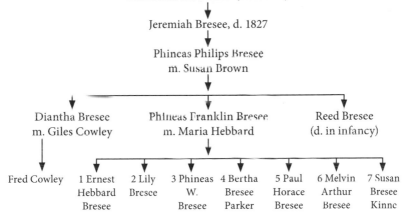

| Diantha Bresee m. Giles Cowley | Phineas Franklin Bresee m. Maria Hebbard | Reed Bresee (d. in infancy) |

| Fred Cowley | 1 Ernest Hebbard Bresee | 2 Lily Bresee | 3 Phineas W. Bresee | 4 Bertha Bresee Parker | 5 Paul Horace Bresee | 6 Melvin Arthur Bresee | 7 Susan Bresee Kinne |

BRESEE'S
ORDINATION TREE

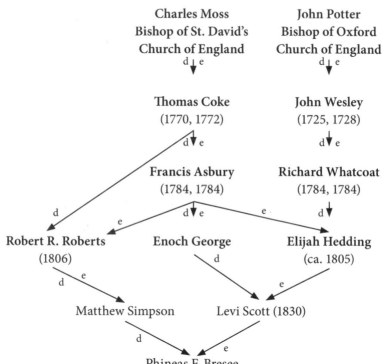

Charles Moss Bishop of St. David's Church of England d ↓ e	**John Potter** Bishop of Oxford Church of England d ↓ e
Thomas Coke (1770, 1772) d ▼ e	**John Wesley** (1725, 1728) d ▼ e
Francis Asbury (1784, 1784) d ▼ e	**Richard Whatcoat** (1784, 1784) d ▼

Robert R. Roberts
(1806)

Enoch George
d

Elijah Hedding
(ca. 1805)

Matthew Simpson

Levi Scott (1830)

Phineas F. Bresee

"d"=deacon
"e"=elder

ABOUT THE AUTHOR

CARL OLIVER BANGS JR. was born
April 5, 1922, in Seattle, Washington, the
only son of immigrants from Norway and
Switzerland. He was raised on his parents' dairy farm and became acquainted
with many pioneer Nazarene leaders on
the West Coast, including H. D. Brown,
Elsie (Mrs. DeLance) Wallace, Alpin M.
Bowes, and H. Orton Wiley. Two of his
sisters (Mildred and Bernice) were also
ordained ministers. He had an early
interest in music and played French horn
in the Seattle Symphony. He was a lifelong member of the Musicians' Union.

His formal study of theology began under Wiley at Pasadena College,
continued under Stephen S. White at Nazarene Theological Seminary, and
Bernard Meland at the University of Chicago, where he received his Ph.D.
degree in 1958. He taught philosophy and religion at Olivet Nazarene College (1953-61) and historical and systematic theology at St. Paul School of
Theology (1961-85).

Bangs was a guest professor at various universities, including the University of Leiden, where Jacobus (James) Arminius taught in the early seventeenth century. Bangs's first major book, *Arminius: A Study in the Dutch
Reformation*, garnered him international renown as an Arminius scholar.
Fourteen other publications also dealt with Arminius and Arminianism—
subjects central to understanding the Reformed theological tradition,
Anglicanism, world Methodism, and American Christianity. Bangs was
president of the Midwest Division of the American Theological Society in
1966 and president of the American Society of Church History in 1972.

211

He enjoyed woodworking and loved hiking the mountains of the Pacific Northwest. He returned as often as possible to Mount Rainier, which he first visited at age four and where his family held frequent reunions.

He was married for nearly sixty years to Marjorie Friesen, whom he met at a church camp in Oregon. She was an accomplished organist and served as his research partner on numerous projects. They raised three children: Carl, Jeremy, and Jeanne. Carl Bangs died on July 7, 2002. Marjorie Bangs died fifteen days later. Their ashes were scattered on Mount Rainer.